The
PIPER
CLASSICS

No. 2457
$19.95

The
PIPER
CLASSICS

Joe Christy

TAB BOOKS Inc.

Blue Ridge Summit, PA

FIRST EDITION

FIRST PRINTING

Copyright © 1988 by TAB BOOKS Inc.

Printed in the United States of America

Reproduction or publication of the content in any manner, without express permission of the publisher, is prohibited. No liability is assumed with respect to the use of the information herein.

Library of Congress Cataloging in Publication Data

Christy, Joe.
   The Piper classics.

   Includes index.
   1. Piper airplanes. I. Title.
TL686.P5C47 1988   629.133′343   87-33511
ISBN 0-8306-9457-9
ISBN 0-8306-2457-0 (pbk.)

Questions regarding the content of this book
should be addressed to:

   Reader Inquiry Branch
   TAB BOOKS Inc.
   Blue Ridge Summit, PA 17294-0214

Cover photograph courtesy of Steven Ogles.

Contents

Introduction

The Piper story begins with the activities of brothers Gilbert and Gordon Taylor of Rochester, New York, in 1928. As almost all others who hoped to become commercial airplane builders during the 1920s, the Taylors had been earning an uncertain living barnstorming. That nomadic existence was expiring—mostly of malnutrition—and experiences with World War I surplus airplanes suggested design improvements that encouraged many ex-barnstormers, including the Taylor brothers, to produce more practical machines for the booming personal airplane market.

It was called the "Lindbergh Boom," it began in 1927, and its proportions can be judged from a single statistic: During the two years immediately following Lindbergh's flight to Paris, student pilot permits jumped from 575 to 20,400 annually. It was popularly said that the Lindbergh flight had "sold" 10,000 airplanes overnight.

Actually, the country was ready for a boom in civil aviation. Lindbergh's dramatic flight was merely the spark that set it off. The Kelly Bill of 1925, which provided for transfer of airmail routes from the Post Office Department to private contractors, gave America a solid foundation for a great domestic airline system. Then, the Air Commerce Act of 1926 established the first air regulations, along with licensing of pilots and aircraft, and brought order and responsibility (and risk capital) to the airways. These advances were followed by the appearance of the first truly reliable and reasonably efficient aircraft engines, the Wright J-5 Whirlwind and the Pratt & Whitney R-1340 Wasp, both of which entered production in 1927.

The Whirlwinds and Wasps powered the machines of the emerging airlines, and allowed a rash of record-breaking flights, including Lindbergh's. After that, until the stock market crashed in October 1929 to begin the Great Depression, there was an abundance of risk capital available for aviation enterprises.

The Taylors' first all-new design (they had extensively modified some surplus Jennies and Standards), a parasol monoplane fitted with a 90-hp five-cylinder Kinner radial engine and seating two side-by-side, was built in 1928. Gordon and a passenger were killed in this airplane early that year, but Gilbert believed in the concept and refused to give up. He went looking for capital.

C. Gilbert Taylor found the investors he needed in the oil town of Bradford, Pennsylvania. The Bradford Board of Commerce gathered a reported $50,000 to capitalize the Taylor Brothers Airplane Company, and several Model B-2 "Chummies" were built in 1929, priced at $3,985, according to Piper records. However, the Taylor Chummy was never certificated, and it's doubted that any were sold before the financial crisis that fall conspired with the Chummy's high price to force its abandonment.

Meanwhile, Taylor stockholder William T. Piper, who had made a little money in oil, convinced Gilbert Taylor that what they needed was a plane that not only would sell for half the Chummy's price, but would also fly for half the Chummy's operations cost. Therefore, by mid-September 1930, Taylor produced a lighter version of the Chummy, fitted with a 20-hp two-cylinder Brownbach engine, called the "Tiger Kitten." This machine, designated the Taylor E-2, was markedly underpowered, however, and the only reason for mentioning the "Tiger Kitten" is that it suggested to Taylor and Piper the name "Cub" for the E-2.

No suitable engine was found for the Taylor Cub at that time, and the company's backers allowed Taylor Brothers Airplane Company to slip into bankruptcy early in 1931. Piper then purchased the E-2 prototype and other company assets for $1,000. Gilbert remained as president and chief engineer of the new Taylor Aircraft Company, probably because he saw little opportunity elsewhere; the Great Depression had not yet reached its low point.

Later that same year, an acceptable engine for the Cub became available, the Continental Motors Corporation A-40, a 37-hp four-cylinder, air-cooled, opposed type that operated on about three gallons of fuel per hour. The A-40 allowed marketing of the E-2 Cub at $1,325, and 24 were sold by the end of 1931.

A total of 134 Cubs were sold through 1934, which were enough to hold the tiny work force together through the Depression's darkest days.

Actually, 30 of the 1934 Cub sales were for the Aeromarine-powered version, which was designated the F-2. The Aeromarine engine, called the AR3-40 as installed in the Cub, was a 50-hp three-cylinder radial, derated to 40 hp by limiting its rpm. Factory price of the F-2 Cub was $1,495.

The year 1935 was the turnaround point for the Cub. Total sales that year were 210, including at least four H-2 versions fitted with the 35-hp three-cylinder Szekely radial (and, perhaps, a prototype G-2 fitted with an engine designed by Gilbert Taylor).

Taylor apparently took a look at the sales figures at that time and decided that what he could do for Piper, he could do for himself. So he left the company, went to Alliance, Ohio (where Wacos were built), and formed the Taylor-Young Aircraft Company. His Taylorcrafts were successfully competing with the Cubs by 1937—but that is another story.

Meanwhile, the Cub was well established in its market. Piper's new chief engineer, Walter C. Jamouneau, slicked up the E-2 with rounded wingtips and vertical tail, wider landing gear, new choice of paints, and the new 40-hp dual-ignition A-40 engine to make the J-2 ("J" for Jamouneau) Cub. Price at the factory was $1,470.

The following year, despite the loss by fire of the Bradford factory, 658 J-2 Cubs were produced, and Piper moved to Lock Haven, Pennsylvania, where the company at last became Piper Aircraft Corporation.

Due to the fire and the move, approximately 100 J-2 "Western Cubs" were built by Aircraft Associates, Inc. in Long Beach, California. The Western Cubs sold for $1,270.

Production at the new facility in Lock Haven began in mid-July 1937, and the first J-3 Piper Cubs were produced there late that year. These were J-3C-40 models fitted with the 40-hp Continental A-40-4. Factory list price was $1,270 for the trainer version, $1,395 for the Sport and $1,895 for the floatplane. Also available was the J-3F-40 with a 40-hp Franklin engine. The 40-hp Cubs were available into 1939, but after the J-3 was certificated with new 50-hp Continental, Franklin, and Lycoming engines in mid-1938, few 40-hp Cubs were built.

The Cub went to 65 hp in 1940, with a choice of Continental, Franklin, or Lycoming powerplants. Prices ranged up to $1,500, depending on equipment. A total of 650 Cubs were built in 1938; 1,400 in 1939; almost 2,000 in 1940; 1,850 in 1941; and 296 in 1942 before wartime priorities stopped production.

After the war, the J-3 was back in production until modified in 1948, when it became the PA-11. Production of the PA-11 ended in 1950, a year after introduction of the PA-18 Super Cub. The Super Cub had wing tanks, flaps, and 90 hp (later, up to 150 hp). Super Cub production trailed off to near zero in the early 1980s, and the design rights were sold by the present-day Piper company to a West Texas firm.

The Piper J-4 Cub Coupe was introduced late in 1938 to compete with the new Taylorcraft and a rash of other light two-placers with side-by-side seating. The J-4 was priced at $1,995 fitted with the 50-hp Continental. The J4-A, which followed in 1939, had 65 hp.

The J-5 series Cub Cruisers, announced in 1940, were three-placers (pilot in front, bench seat for two in back) with a 75-hp Continental or Lycoming. The J-5C had the new 100-hp O-235 Lycoming. Piper built 495 Cruisers in 1940, 870 in 1941, and perhaps 60 in 1942. A modified J-5, powered with the 125-hp Lycoming O-290-C, was the YL-14 for the Army. Only a handful of YL-14s were built. Most Cubs built for the Army were J-3 variants designated L-4s.

After the war, the three-place Piper PA-12 Super Cruiser entered production in February 1946, and more than 3,500 were sold before production ended early in 1948. Initially powered by the 100-hp Lycoming O-235-C, most were fitted with the 108-hp O-235-C1.

Replacing the PA-12 in April 1948, the PA-14 Family Cruiser appeared with four seats; at $3,985, it was the lowest-priced four-placer in the market. It was powered with the 108-hp O-235-C1, and 237 were manufactured before the postwar civil lightplane market was saturated and the entire industry was forced to cut back production.

Meanwhile, at the end of World War II, Piper tested a little single-place airplane, the Skycycle, which it hoped to sell for $995. The major portion of its fuselage was a surplus external drop tank made for Navy F4U Corsair fighters. The Skycycle's engine was a Lycoming O-145-A rated at 55 hp. It had a wingspan of 20 feet and cruised at 95 mph, but like the PA-6 Skysedan (and, 10 years later, the two-place Papoose), the Skycycle was abandoned.

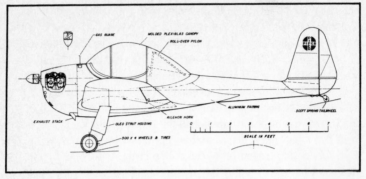

The Piper Skycycle was planned to sell for less than $1,000 in the post-World War II market. The engine was the 65-hp Lycoming; the main fuselage was adapted from a war surplus belly tank. The Skycycle was flown in prototype only. (courtesy James Triggs)

It was the little two-place PA-15 Vagabond that rescued Piper from the doldrums. The no-frills Vag, powered by the 65-hp Lycoming and priced at $1,990, appeared in mid-1948. About 500 found buyers—and Piper craftsmen were back to work. The Vagabond was the first of the now-popular "short wing" Pipers, and the PA-15 was almost immediately followed by the PA-17, a deluxe version of the PA-15, which was powered with the 65-hp Continental. The PA-17 sold for $2,195 at the factory, and at least 200 were built. Many Vagabonds still flying today have larger engines—which is a sign of the times, rather than one of need.

The Piper Clipper, PA-16, evolved from the Vagabonds early in 1949. The Clipper is, essentially, a four-place Vagabond with almost twice the power. Its production life was short, but it justified the Piper Pacer and Tri-Pacer, highly successful designs. The Clipper's engine was the 115-hp Lycoming O-235-C1.

The Piper Pacer, PA-20, was introduced in 1950, and 1128 were built during the two years it was in production. It began life with the 115-hp Lycoming, but only a few of those were sold before a switch was made to the 125-hp Lycoming O-290-D. Later, the Pacer was offered with the 135-hp O-290-D2. Most were 125-hp. The Pacer would provide the airframe for the Tri-Pacers and Colts to follow. The 135-hp Pacer, by the way, was equipped with an Aeromatic or Sensenich controllable-pitch propeller.

The Piper Tri-Pacer, PA-22, entered the market in 1952, and remained in production throughout the 1950s and into early 1963. The early Tri-Pacers came with the O-290-D Lycoming, then the 135-hp O-290-D2. By 1959, the Caribbean model of the PA-22 was powered with the 150-hp Lycoming O-320, while the Standard and Super Custom Tri-Pacers were equipped with the Lycoming O-320-B rated at 160 hp. The 1959 Caribbean sold for $8,395. The deluxe version of the Caribbean was $1,000 more, and possessed a 12-channel Narco Superhomer, position lights, wheel pants, strut cuffs, attitude gyro, and a few other minor goodies. The 1959 Standard Tri-Pacer, 160-hp, had a list price of $8,890, while the Super Custom, with radios and full panel, was priced at $10,770.

The Piper Colt, PA-22-108, appeared in 1960, and was built for a couple of years—partly, it was said, to use up stockpiled materials intended for the discontinued Tri-Pacer series, and partly to hold Piper's two-place economy market until the new low-wing Cherokee could establish itself in the four-place market. Then, the Cherokee could be reconfigured as a two-placer, among other things. Also, the proposed two-place Papoose was under consideration at the time.

The Colt was powered with the 108-hp Lycoming O-235-C1B. It was intended as a trainer, and served reasonably well. When production ended for the PA-22 series early in 1963, more than 7,600 Tri-Pacers and Colts had been built.

The Piper Papoose was planned as a low-cost sport trainer of composite construction during the late 1950s. It was never produced. (courtesy Piper Aircraft)

These are the fun Pipers. They were designed and built in a simple, uncomplicated manner to provide safe flying at minimum cost to the average private pilot. The owner/pilots of these aircraft today aren't out to prove anything with their airplanes. They simply love to fly, and they have an ideal machine for that purpose—and unless you have flown a Vagabond from a small, grass field on a crisp, dewey-fresh spring morning, you are in no position to argue that point.

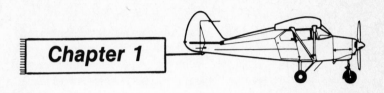

Chapter 1

The Piper Cubs—
J-3, PA-11, and PA-18

The Piper J-3 Cub was a child of the Great Depression. It—and a handful of light monoplanes that shared its design philosophy—became very popular during the late 1930s, originally because they reduced the cost of flying to a bare minimum, and later because they were the machines of the Civilian Pilot Training Program. On the little sod field from which I flew every week, solo time was $7 per hour after the Cubs and Taylorcrafts appeared. Prior to that, the price had been $20 per hour for the Spartan C-3 or Travel Air E-4000 biplanes—$24 per hour for dual instruction.

It had taken almost three years for me to solo the Travel Air. Most of that time I was in high school and earning $1 per day in my part-time job, so I had to buy dual instruction in 30-minute chunks, often a couple of months apart. However, things moved a little faster once my friend Clarence obtained his private pilot certificate. Then, each of us could put up $5 and Clarence could officially log a half-hour, while I learned to fly—sort of.

Of course, it was illegal, but it was widely done during those lean times. There was no minimum requirement for solo. You soloed when your instructor decided that you were ready, and I never heard of anyone exceeding the standard eight hours of dual that was considered adequate. Three to five hours of dual officially logged was enough to solo some people, usually because they had somewhat more than that in "bootleg" air time. In any case, the Cubs and T-Crafts and Aeroncas changed all that by the end of the 1930s.

THE CIVILIAN PILOT TRAINING PROGRAM

Other things had also changed by then, including an improving economy due to the outbreak of war in Europe. England and France were buying war supplies in America, which created jobs. The war also forced the U.S. to begin to look to its own shaky defenses, and one of the results of that was the Civilian Pilot Training Program (CPTP), which provided free flight training to college students.

The U.S. Congress and the colleges/universities were persuaded to accept the CPTP because it was presented as a purely civilian program, administered by the newly-created Civil Aeronautics Authority (CAA), and was intended to aid the private flying industry in general, and the struggling fixed-base flight operators in particular. More or less as an afterthought, it was sometimes mentioned that a large pool of recently trained pilots in the 18-to-25-year age group might be useful if the war in Europe should (God forbid!) somehow engulf the U.S. It seems clear that, without that threat, the CPTP would not have been instituted.

Whether or not the CPTP was really intended for doves or hawks, it turned out to be the most successful program ever

A Piper J-2 fitted with a Glen Angle 5-60 radial engine. Except for the rudder and fin, the basic Cub shape was firmed up with appearance of the J-2. (courtesy Emil Strasser)

conceived by the CAA or its successor FAAs. The CPTP Act became law on June 27, 1939, and the first 330 students began training in 13 colleges. When the program ended in the summer of 1944, 1,132 colleges and universities had been involved, and 435,165 student pilots—including several hundred women—received private pilot certificates after training with 1,460 FBOs. The CAA administered the program with surprising efficiency, and in most cases managed to hold payments to the contracting FBOs to $6 per hour for the 35 to 50 hours allowed each student. Seldom has the American taxpayer received so much for his money.

While training more than 435,000 student pilots, the CAA's program resulted in fewer than 100 fatalities—a record so unbelievable at the time that the CAA was accused of withholding accident information.

There were several good reasons for the CPTP's excellent safety record: (1) the target cost of $6 per hour, but in training airplanes with no less than 50 hp, mandated that the aircraft be Cubs, Taylorcrafts, Aeroncas, and their clones; (2) the schools tended to pick serious applicants; and (3) the flight course was standardized—the same at every airport. The 72-hour ground course was also stylized at all the colleges.

Gradually, the CPTP felt the pressures of the developing world crisis, and CAA policy became increasingly influenced by the military. In the summer of 1941, women were no longer accepted, and a

Piper J-3F-50 was built through 1939 and was powered with the 50-hp Franklin engine. This one belonged to famed aerobatic and movie pilot Tex Rankin. Photographed at Payette, Washington. (courtesy Peter M. Bowers)

The Piper J-3C-50 was fitted with the 50-hp Continental engine. Airshow pilot Mike Murphy took off and landed on grass fields with this float-equipped version. (courtesy Emil Strasser)

military pledge was required for participation. Then, a few days after the attack on Pearl Harbor, President Roosevelt ordered that the CPTP be devoted exclusively to military training, and shortly after that its name was changed to the War Training Service (WTS).

At least 10,000 airplanes were used in the CPTP/WTS. Approximately three-fourths of the trainees took their flight instruction in Cubs; but other light monoplanes were also used, as previously noted, along with a mélange of ex-civilian aircraft. Except for 132 Waco cabin biplanes built for the WTS after Pearl Harbor, no other civilian airplanes were produced during the war years. Soon, replacement parts became a problem, and the WTS flight contractors found themselves increasingly short of planes.

Everything had to be procured on a priority basis. Obtaining a priority was problem enough, but when the War Production Board issued one, it was little more than a "hunting license." By 1943 the situation had become so desperate that the War Production Board issued a freeze order that halted the sale, lease, rental, trade, or delivery of any airplane to anyone other than the Defense Plant Corporation. The order covered all single-engine civilian planes up to 500 hp.

The Defense Plant Corporation then bought every such aircraft it could find, from WTS operators and other sources. Between March and August 1943, 5,441 airplanes were purchased. Then the Defense Plant Corporation leased the machines to the CAA, which in turn subleased them to the flight schools. The Defense Plant

The J-3 Cub fitted with a 50-hp three-cylinder radial Lenape Papoose engine was certificated as the J-3P-50. (courtesy Emil Strasser)

Corporation, a government entity, could get parts and, through the CAA, see to it that whoever needed training planes got them. It was a typically bureaucratic way of doing things, but it seemed to work okay.

The CAA's annual report for 1944 provides some interesting details on the WTS aircraft, stating that 7,585 were used in that phase of the program—1,401 privately owned and 6,177 government-owned. Of the latter, 5,170 belonged to the Defense Plant Corporation, 533 to the Navy, and 474 to the Army. These figures include 781 machines of 226-to-500 hp, 632 of 146-to-225 hp, 462 of 90-to-145 hp, and 5,703 in the 50-to-89 hp range, the majority of the last category being Piper Cubs.

The J-3 Cub was the workhorse of the CPTP/WTS. Four out of five trainees won their wings in it, and according to the FAA, three out of four combat pilots in World War II "learned their ABCs in it."

The military services operated Cubs in almost every theater of war, and these aircraft served in many capacities, including artillery fire direction, transport, reconnaissance, ambulance, mail delivery, and general "gofer." In some invasion operations, Cubs were launched from landing-ship tanks (LSTs). During the invasion of Normandy, more than 1,000 Cubs were flown from England to fields in France. In other actions, many were shipped into combat zones in cargo planes and assembled at the scene of operation. One could compile a very long book of shooting-type war stories involving the gentle, pokey Cub.

USAAF CUBS

The U.S. Army Air Forces took delivery of 4,788 Piper observation/liaison airplanes during World War II. The first ones, 144 in number, were O-59s ("O" for observation, redesignated "L" for liaison in 1942). The O-59s later became L-4s, and 649 originally O-59As were later redesignated L-4As, along with 299 delivered from Piper as L-4As. These were the same as the J-3s fitted with the 65-hp Continental (J-3C-65).

The USAAF received 981 of the L-4B, which was the same as the L-4A but without radio. Delivered to the Army were 10 L-4Cs (J-3L-65), 5 L-4Ds (J-3F-65), 16 L-4Es (J-4E), 45 L-4Fs (J-5A), 41 L-4Gs (J-5B), 1,801 L-4Hs (65-hp Lycoming O-170-3 engine), and 1,680 L-4Js (same as L-4Hs but with controllable propeller). Five L-14s, which were modified J-5s fitted with the 125-hp Lycoming O-290D engine, were delivered, and an order for 845 more was cancelled on VJ Day.

POSTWAR CUBS

In 1947, the Piper PA-11 Cub Special appeared. This airplane was essentially the J-3 with a full cowling and its fuel tank moved to the left wing root. The PA-11 was briefly offered with a 65-hp Continental engine, but most were produced with the Continental C-90.

The Special's fuel capacity was increased to 18 gallons, and a small header tank remained behind the firewall. This craft was soloed from the front seat (the J-3s were soloed from the rear), and some were rigged for crop spraying, although they could carry only 400 pounds of pesticide.

Super Cubs

The PA-18 Super Cub was announced in 1949, and it probably should not be included with the "fun" Pipers because most Super Cubs work for a living. One version, built in 1950-1951, with 125 hp, was procured by the U.S Army as the L-21.

The Super Cub has been offered with just about every certificated aircraft engine from the 90-hp Continental to the 150-hp Lycoming O-320. This airplane is not a modified J-3. Despite the fact that it very much resembles the J-3 and PA-11, its airframe

The unusual markings on this 1939 model J-3C-50 Cub probably indicate that it was one of the Cubs purchased by the government during World War II and leased back to a civilian operator for the War Training Service. (courtesy Peter M. Bowers)

incorporates a number of structural changes. The first PA-18s sold for $3,595 and $4,295—90 and 125 hp, respectively—but by the time Super Cub production finally ended (they were built on order into the early 1980s), they were priced above $30,000.

The Super Cub models were designed for a number of jobs such as glider towing, pipeline patrol, banner towing, and agricultural work. The 125-hp Super Cub could take off in about 140 feet and, with flaps, could be slowed to about 33 mph in the air. Model PA-18A was the special duster/sprayer version introduced in 1951. The PA-18A left the factory with a 110-gallon chemical hopper and other special features, such as wire cutters on the landing gear legs, a removable metal belly, and reinforced loading areas.

DAVE BLANTON ON TAILWHEEL LANDING GEAR

If you don't know David Blanton, you are missing one of the rewards of being an airplane person. Dave is president of Javelin Aircraft, located on the Augusta (Kansas) Municipal Airport on the east edge of Wichita. Javelin is an engineering firm that solves special problems for the Wichita aircraft manufacturers and, as time permits, works on innovations of its own, such as converting Ford automobile engines to aircraft use. Anyway, when I told Dave about *The Piper Classics* book project, he favored me with a fine dissertation on the subject of tailwheel airplanes. You must understand that Dave holds very positive views on most aeronautical topics:

This J-3 Cub, powered with the 65-hp Continental engine, was photographed on May 4, 1959 in Ontario, Canada. (courtesy Peter M. Bowers)

A J-3 floatplane fitted with the 65-hp Continental engine in flight over Cabrillo Beach, California, 1957. (courtesy Peter M. Bowers)

"I'm glad you brought that up," he said, leaning forward, elbows on his desk. "The tailwheel of an airplane with dynamically unstable main landing gear is serious business. In motion, it's like trying to shoot an arrow feather-end first. The center of gravity is behind the main gear, so any side load will cause the airplane to want to swap ends. The resulting maneuver is called a ground loop. The pilot must be trained and experienced to manually overcome the dynamic instability of such a landing gear.

"In past years, many airplanes had full-swivel tailwheels. Examples can be seen on the Stinson Reliant, Beech 17, and Wacos. Some of these airplanes had lousy mechanical brakes, and some had heel brakes or a big 'Johnson bar' lever. The old Tri-Motor Ford had mechanical brakes actuated by a bar about four feet long, which was operated by the copilot as the pilot screamed instructions.

"The best insurance against destroying a tailwheel airplane with a ground loop is a locking tailwheel. In recent years, most aircraft of this configuration have gone to hydraulic toe brakes and steerable tailwheels. This ends the problem—if the pilot is halfway competent.

"A PT-17 Stearman is the world's best at ground looping. If there is an incompetent pilot in the driver's seat, he is going to go for a ride. The landing gear is narrow, and all of the fuel is in the top wing. If it swings five degrees, and the pilot just sits there with his brain up and locked and doesn't do anything, it's going to go around. If it's going left, he can slowly bring on right rudder with no effect. He can jam on the right brake and it will go backwards, around the right wheel.

"Every time you are on final to land a tailwheel airplane, you should tell yourself: (a) I'm trying to shoot an arrow feather-end first; (b) I must get the stick back and keep it back to prevent a porpoise and to get the tailwheel on the ground so that I can manually steer with it to overcome the dynamic instability of this type landing gear; and (c) Look to see where the wind is. It's generally to the left or right. Put the wing down into the wind to compensate for drift. There is no need to land on both main wheels at the same time. The upwind wheel should always touch first... .

"Years ago, I landed on the old Kansas City Municipal Airport in my Stinson Boiler. Someone had put automotive fluid in the brakes because it used automotive master cylinders—the system required red fluid—and as a result, everything was gummed up. I tried to do everything right, but stopped headed straight west on the main north-south runway. I'll never forget the guy in the tower. He said, 'Now, you can taxi three hundred feet north to an intersection to get off the runway, or you can taxi three hundred feet south to an intersection and get off the runway.'

"The tricycle landing gear is dynamically stable and wants to go straight. Don't ever let a person who has flown only tricycle-gear airplanes fly your tailwheel aircraft. I guarantee that he will tear it up.

"To me, it's irritating to hear the expression 'taildragger.' That

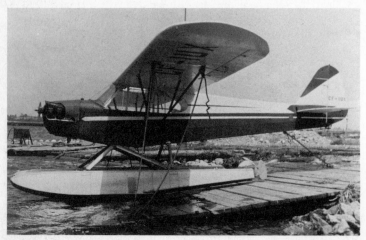

Canadian J-3 floatplane, registered CF-IUX. (courtesy Ken Molson)

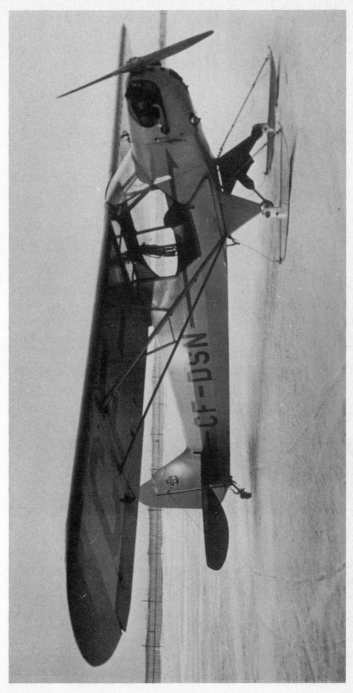

A postwar J-3 in Canadian livery, photographed March 27, 1947. (courtesy Joseph P. Juptner)

11

is a flippant term from irresponsible people lacking in a true aviation background... .

"When one is checking out in a tailwheel airplane, it is best not to try to 'grease it on' when landing. Learn to drop it that last six inches. You can grease it on later, when you know what you are doing. The reason for dropping the airplane six inches is that the airspeed at touchdown will be 5 to 10 mph less, which is 10 to 20 percent of stalling speed. But the difference in dynamics to cause a ground loop will be 50 percent less. If you drop it on three-point, the airplane will have only one-half the dynamic energy to cause a ground loop, as compared to trying to grease it on and letting the forward wheels touch first. The dynamics vary with the square of the speed."

"I agree with you," I said. "Keep the stick back once you're on the ground, and stay sharp on the rudder pedals. I learned to fly in airplanes with tailskids."

It was evident that Dave approved of that, and he continued, switching the subject to wheel landings in tailwheel airplanes.

"Keeping the airspeed up, and rolling the forward wheels on the ground in level attitude, can result in a nice landing in some airplanes, particularly in high winds. But what can happen to the uninitiated in this scenario? The pilot may not know what his minimum airspeed must be to land on the wheels in level flight. Or, he tries

Nebraska pilot Jeff Clausen (with his like-new J-3) provides us with a gem of a story, "A Cowboy and His Airplane," in this chapter. (courtesy Jeff Clausen)

The PA-18 Super Cub appeared in 1949. The first ones offered had 90/95 hp, but they would eventually employ most available engines through 150 hp. The Super Cub could be a fun airplane, but most worked for a living.

this in a no-wind condition and has enough dynamics in the airplane not only to tear up the airplane, but half the airport, too. This happens somewhere every day. Then, we are all forced to listen to all the dumb excuses as to why.

"The FAA cries about ground loop accidents, but the FAA people involved don't know enough about flying to know how to prevent them. Most FAA-certificated instructors are strong on playing with radios, but really don't know much about stick-and-rudder flying.

"It's important to have a good steerable tailwheel with good strong steering springs. But all this good hardware is worthless unless the pilot will get the stick back and keep it there. If the pilot will keep the airplane rolling straight on landing with a steerable tailwheel, he won't ground loop. If the tailwheel shimmies and unlocks, then the only thing that will save the situation are the toe brakes.

"Now, what will cause the tailwheel to shimmy? The pivot axis must be forward at the bottom three-to-six degrees at gross weight. If it is not, disassemble the tail spring, re-arch one leaf at a time on an arbor press, and reassemble it. Do not use rubber of any kind; use metal-to-metal and bolt it solid. You should be very careful to keep the tailwheel in good condition; it is the cheapest insurance you can buy for your tailwheel airplane."

A COWBOY AND HIS AIRPLANE

Meanwhile, not all aviation people approach flying with the same attitude, as Jeff Clausen, of Lincoln, Nebraska, will testify. Jeff's following account of a Super Cub pilot originally appeared in the *Short Wing Piper News*, the official publication of the Short Wing Piper Club, Inc.

Old Fred, as he was known around the airport, was a rancher who owned a 1959 Super Cub; bought it new. Old Fred learned how to fly back in 1946, just after the war, in a J-3 Cub. His nephew had been an Army Air Forces instructor during the war, and came to help Fred on the ranch one summer. He taught Fred the basics of aerodynamics and eventually let him solo.

Old Fred had been flying about 25 years when I met him. He would come buzzing the field in his gray-and-green Super Cub with gaudy flourescent-orange wingtips and land in front of the hangar on the taxiway. He would take me flying with him quite often, especially when he went to some other town. I thought it was great because I got to fly the Super Cub and log the time as pilot-in-command because I had my private license. Well, after about a year of this I discovered that Old Fred had nothing but a student permit that had expired 20 years ago. That didn't bother me much, because I was doing the flying anyway. What did get my attention, however, was the fact that Old Fred got his airplane

Super Cub cockpit. The throttle knob is visible just above the seat back, on the left side of the cabin.

"annualed" once every five or six years whether it needed it or not. Living out in the boonies, one doesn't worry much about Uncle Friendly snooping around, grounding airplanes.

On this particular summer day, Old Fred decided his plane should have its annual inspection, as it was 1970 and the last time a mechanic had looked at it was 1964. Besides, the cows got out and ate the fabric off the left side of the fuselage, and it got a little windy for Old Fred.

My boss and I started work on the Super Cub. The fabric was totally shot, but Fred wanted only the big hole repaired. The fabric punched out at 40 pounds (legal minimum is 56 pounds tensile strength per square inch), but Fred figured it was good for another ten years. My boss didn't mind, as Fred lost the airplane's logbooks years ago and nothing was ever recorded.

I was draining the oil, and Fred came up and asked just what in the heck I was doing. He said he changed the oil every ten days or so and to put that oil back in the engine. What he meant was that, since the engine had over 2000 hours on it, he'd burn about one and a-half quarts every hour, and therefore the oil was "changed" every four or five hours. He went on to inform me that Aeroshell was too damned expensive. He used Pennzoil, Valvoline, Phillips 66, and combinations of all three, as that was cheaper, and that's what his tractors used.

After about a week of working on Fred's airplane, I was glad to see it go. I cleaned about 75 shotgun shells out of the back, dozens of mouse nests (including five little mice) out of the wings, a pair of pliers from under the stick, two quarts of Valvoline that were wedged way back in the fuselage, 87¢ in loose change, enough grass and hay to feed a large horse, three hornet nests, and roughly five acres of topsoil.

When Fred paid his bill, he was cursing about the cost, and muttering to himself about waiting ten years instead of five to get his next annual. He was a good ol' boy, though; he'd curse and talk tough, but he was usually a teddy bear. He flew people to and from their ranches when the weather got bad and would air-drop supplies when the roads were impassable.

My fondest memory of Old Fred was the time he flew in and wanted me to show him how to use his radio. After showing him how the VOR worked, he was simply amazed. He was even more amazed when I showed him an Omaha Sectional. Why, it not only depicted where the airport was located, it even gave field elevation and runway length!

Getting Fred to talk on the radio correctly was a challenge. He had the old coffee-grinder-style radio and could never get the hang of it. He would speak into the mike, then hold it up to his ear, thinking that's where the sound was coming from. I gave him an old pair of headphones, and Fred was just awed over that new technology.

One nice Sunday morning, Fred decided to fly his wife to Lincoln so she could visit with relatives for a week. On the Saturday before the big trip, I tried to explain the correct procedure for landing at Lincoln.

Champion aerobatic pilot Charlie Hillard began his airshow career in this clipped-wing Cub. (courtesy Harold Krier collection)

Charlie Hillard of Ft. Worth and Harold Krier of Wichita brush wingtips in a head-on pass at an airshow. Hillard's clipped-wing Cub was originally STCed by old barnstormer Earl Reed of Kansas City. (courtesy Harold Krier collection)

17

Fred had never landed at a controlled field, so he was a little apprehensive. Since he couldn't get the hang of tuning his VHT-3, I set the frequency on 118.5 for him, told him not to touch it, and advised him to tell the tower he wanted to stay on 118.5 for taxi instructions.

Early Sunday morning, Old Fred and his wife departed for Lincoln. He was really feeling good about his trip, as he had all the latest innovations on board—his VHT-3, headphones, and an Omaha Sectional. All week the weather had been lousy, so on Sunday it was beautiful and everyone was out flying at Lincoln Municipal. I had tried to talk Fred into landing at Arrow Airport, but his wife's relatives lived closer to Muni and didn't know how to get to Arrow, so it was the big airport for Fred.

Anyway, he found Lincoln, and about 25 miles out his radio came to life, and everyone was talking so much and so fast Fred couldn't get a word in edgewise, let alone understand what was said.

About this time, Fred was getting a little nervous as the airport was getting closer and closer, and he saw three or four other airplanes in the sky. Out in the boonies, if you see one airplane in a hundred-mile radius, you log it as formation flying.

About ten miles out, Fred was completely baffled, what with all the chatter and all the airplanes in and around the airport. Then it dawned on him . . . Old Fred all of a sudden had a plan. He picked up the mike and as soon as there was a pause in the chatter, he blurted out in an excited voice, "Lincoln Tower, this is eight-five-six-four-Charlie. Clear the runway! I'm going to try to bring this thing in on one engine!"

The Army's L-21 had flaps, a greenhouse, and 125 hp. This one had been declared surplus and transferred to Ft. Sill's Redleg Flying Club in the early 1960s.

There was silence for about five seconds, then the tower responded, "Roger, six-four-Charlie, understand you're bringing it in on one engine. Cleared to land on any runway you choose."

Old Fred smiled all the way down on final as all the other lightplanes scattered to get out of the way and the controllers searched the sky with binoculars for the big twin. Fred did as he always did back home. He landed on the taxiway in front of the hangar.

As soon as he got out of his Cub, the lineboy walked up and said the tower would like to talk with him. But Fred lucked out with nothing more than a severe reprimand and an invitation never to come to Lincoln again.

I haven't seen Old Fred for many years now. I hope when I go home this Christmas, I run into him out at the airport. Maybe, after all these years, he'll bring his Super Cub in for another annual.

CUB CONSTRUCTION

The J-3 fuselage framework was built of welded chrome moly steel tubing (4130 and 1025), lightly faired to shape and covered with Grade A cotton fabric, testing 80 psi, warp and fill, minimum. Flightex was the most widely used brand name. The finish on the original Cubs was cellulose nitrate dope. Postwar Cubs were finished with cellulose butyrate dope. The last Super Cubs were covered with Ceconite Dacron cloth.

Seats of 26-inch width were mounted in tandem, and a large split-type door opened most of the right side; the airplane could be (and often was) flown with the right side open. Windshield and windows were of Pyralin, and the left-side window was slidable for controlled ventilation. The sparse upholstery was whipcord; a small baggage shelf behind the rear seat had a 20-pound capacity. The nine-gallon (or optional 12-gallon) fuel tank was mounted just behind the firewall and utilized a simple, bobber-type fuel gauge that projected through the filler cap. The wing was framed with solid spruce spars (early models) or dural spars (late models) and stamped aluminum ribs. The leading edges, back to the front spar, were covered with dural metal sheet, and the completed framework was fabric-covered.

A simple tripod landing gear of 72-inch tread was snubbed with Rusco rubber shock rings, and the 7.00 × 4 wheels were shod with low-pressure tires. There were no wheel brakes on the early Cubs, except as extra-cost items. The fabric-covered tail group was framed

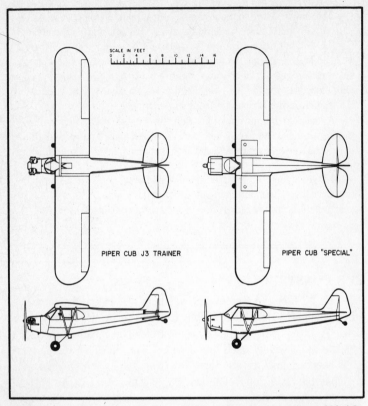

PIPER CUB J3 TRAINER

PIPER CUB "SPECIAL"

Profile views of the Piper J-3 Cub and PA-11 Special. More than 1000 J-3s were produced after World War II; they were replaced by the PA-11 in 1947, which was in turn replaced by the PA-18 in 1949.

of welded steel tube, and the horizontal stabilizer was adjusted in flight, controlled by a jack screw. The rudder was aerodynamically balanced, and all controls were operated by twisted steel cable.

The standard J-3 finish was "Cub Yellow" (Randolph M-9521-D Sport Yellow) with black trim. A Sensenich wooden propeller, wiring for position lights, dual controls, safety belts, and a first aid kit were standard equipment. Optional equipment included battery, position lights, carburetor heater, cabin heater, steerable tailwheel, Goodyear air wheels with brakes, 12-gallon fuel tank, wheel pants, prop spinner, Edo 1070 floats, and skis. The Goodyear tire size was 8.00 × 4.

Approximately 900 J-3 Cubs were produced in 1945, 1,320 in 1946, and 720 in 1947. There were 1,400 PA-11s built from 1947 through 1950.

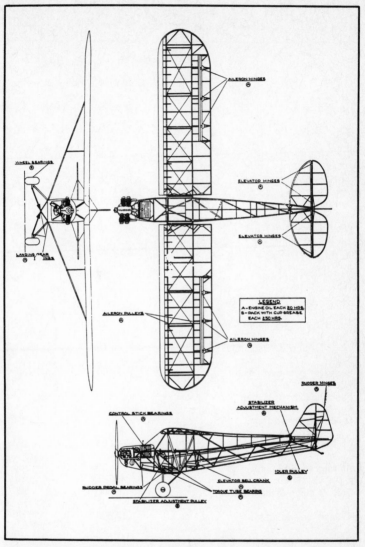

All of the fabric-covered Pipers had fuselages framed of chrome moly steel tubing; tail surface frames were also of welded steel tubing. Wings had stamped metal ribs with spruce spars until early 1941, when extruded dural spars were substituted. Until 1943 all (except the last PA-18s) were covered with aircraft-grade cotton fabric, finished in cellulose nitrate dope. In that year the finish was changed to cellulose acetate butyrate dope. (courtesy Piper Aircraft Corp.)

Piper J-3 Cub
Specifications and Performance

	J-3C-50	J-3P-50
Engine	Cont A-50	Papoose L-200
Hp and rpm.	50 @ 1900	50 @ 2200
Gross weight (lbs.).	1100	1100
Empty weight (lbs.).	635	630
Useful load (lbs.).	465	470
Wingspan (ft.).	35.25	35.25
Wing area (sq. ft.).	178	178
Length (ft.).	22.25	22.3
Height (in.).	80	80
Chord (in.).	63	63
Power loading (lbs./hp).	22	22
Wing loading (lbs./sq. ft.).	6.18	6.18
Baggage capacity (lbs.).	20	20
Fuel capacity (U.S. gal.).	12	12
Maximum speed (mph).	90	92
Cruise (mph).	80	80
Stalling speed (mph).	35	35
Rate of climb (initial; ft./min.).	500	500
Service ceiling (ft.).	10,000	12,000
Cruising range (statute mi.).	250	270
Fuel consumption (gal./hr.).	3.5	3.5

Piper J-3 Cub and Taylor E-2 Cub
Specifications and Performance

	J-3C-65	E-2
Engine	Cont A-65-8	Cont A-40-2
Hp and rpm.....................	65 @ 2300	37 @ 2550
Gross weight (lbs.)...............	1220	925
Empty weight (lbs.)...............	680	532
Useful load (lbs.).................	540	393
Wingspan (ft.)....................	35.25	35.25
Wing area (sq. ft.)................	178.5	184
Length (ft.)......................	22.4	22.25
Height (in.)......................	80	78
Propeller (max. in.)...............	72	- -
Power loading (lbs./hp)............	18.75	25
Wing loading (lbs./sq. ft.).........	6.84	5.03
Baggage capacity (lbs.)...........	20	- -
Fuel capacity (U.S. gal.)...........	12	9
Maximum speed (mph)............	87	70
Cruise (mph @ 3000 ft.)..........	73	62
Stalling speed (mph)..............	38	28
Rate of climb (ft./min.)............	450	400
Service ceiling (ft.)...............	11,500	12,000
Cruising range (statute mi.)........	220	180
Glide ratio......................	10:1	12:1
Fuel consumption (gal./hr.).........	4.08	2.7

Piper Cub Special (PA-11-65 and PA-11-90)
Specifications and Performance

	PA-11-65	PA-11-90
Engine	Cont A-65-8/9	Cont C-90
Hp and rpm	65 @ 2300	90 @ 2475
Gross weight (lbs.)	1220	1220
Empty weight (lbs.)	730	750
Useful load (lbs.)	490	470
Wingspan (ft.)	35.25	35.25
Wing area (sq. ft.)	178.5	178.5
Length (ft.)	22.4	22.4
Height (in.)	80	80
Propeller diameter (in.)	72	72
Power loading (lbs./hp)	18.7	13.5
Wing loading (lbs./sq. ft.)	6.9	6.9
Baggage capacity (lbs.)	20	20
Fuel capacity (U.S. gal.)	18	18
Maximum speed (mph)	100	112
Cruise (mph @ 3000 ft.)	87	100
Stalling speed (mph)	38	40
Rate of climb (initial; ft./min.)	514	900
Service ceiling (ft.)	14,000	16,000
Absolute ceiling (ft.)	16,000	18,000
Cruising range (statute mi.)	300	350
Fuel consumption (gal./hr.)	4.7	5
Best rate of climb speed (mph)	55	55
Takeoff run (ft.)	350	250

Piper Super Cub (PA-18)
Specifications and Performance

	PA-18-90	PA-18-108
Engine	Cont C-90	Lyc O-235
Hp and rpm.	90 @ 2475	108 @ 2600
Gross weight (lbs.).	1300	1340
Empty weight (lbs.).	840	875
Useful load (lbs.).	460	465
Wingspan (ft.).	35.3	35.3
Wing area (sq. ft.).	178.5	178.5
Length (ft.).	22.4	22.4
Height (in.).	79	79
Propeller diameter (in.).	74	74
Power loading (lbs./hp).	14.4	12.5
Wing loading (lbs./sq. ft.).	7.3	7.5
Baggage capacity.	none	none
Fuel capacity (U.S. gal.).	18	18
Maximum speed (mph).	112	117
Cruising speed (mph).	100	105
Stalling speed (mph).	42	42
Rate of climb (initial; ft./min.).	700	850
Service ceiling (ft.).	15,000	17,500
Absolute ceiling (ft.).	18,000	19,500
Fuel consumption (gal./hr.).	5	7
Cruising range (statute mi.).	360	270
Takeoff run (ft.).	400	350

Piper Super Cub PA-18
Specifications and Performance

	PA-18-125	PA-18-150
Engine	Lyc O-290-D	Lyc O-320-A2A
Hp and rpm	125 @ 2600	150 @ 2700
Gross weight (lbs.)	1500	1750
Empty weight (lbs.)	845	930
Useful load (lbs.)	655	820
Wingspan (ft.)	35.3	35.4
Wing area (sq. ft.)	178.5	178.5
Length (ft.)	22.4	22.6
Height (in.)	79	80
Power loading (lbs./hp)	12	13.9
Wing loading (lbs./sq. ft.)	8.4	10
Propeller diameter (in.)	- -	74
Baggage capacity (lbs.)	50	50
Fuel capacity (U.S. gal.)	18	36
Maximum speed (mph)	125	130
Cruise (mph; 75% power)	110	115
Stalling speed (mph)	38*	43*
Takeoff run (ft.)	210*	200*
Landing roll (ft.)	300*	350*
Climb rate (initial; ft./min.)	1000	960
Service ceiling (ft.)	19,500	19,000
Cruising range (statute mi.)	250	460

*Flaps extended.

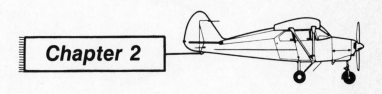

Chapter 2

The Piper
Coupes and Cruisers

The J-4 series Coupes were clearly meant to directly compete with the rash of light monoplane two-placers with side-by-side seating that followed the first Taylorcraft into the market. That first T-Craft, along with the Aeronca K, were certificated by mid-1937. Within a couple of years, there were at least four T-Craft models, six Aeroncas, two Luscombes, a Funk, and a Rearwin—all two-place, with side-by-side seating, and with engines ranging from 40 hp to 75 hp.

THE J-4 SERIES

The first J-4 Cub Coupe was announced in September 1938. It was equipped with the 50-hp Continental and sold for $1,995, which was $500 more than the 50-hp T-Craft Model BC. However, the Coupe possessed, as standard equipment, hydraulic wheel brakes, cabin heater, wheel pants, fire extinguisher, position lights, propeller spinner, first aid kit, and a hand-rubbed finish, all of which were normally extra-cost items.

In mid-1939, the Cub Coupe acquired the 65-hp Continental engine to become the J-4A Model. The J-4A had a fully cowled engine, while the cylinders were exposed on the J-4 Coupe. The Coupes had an entry door on both sides of the cabin and sliding

The Cub J-4 Coupe had side-by-side seating for two, and 50 or 65 hp. This machine was introduced in the late summer of 1938 and was originally priced at $1,995. (courtesy William Larkin)

windows. Controls were dual stick, with a centrally mounted throttle. Fuel was carried in a 16-gallon tank in the right wing root. A nine-gallon auxiliary tank was optional and located in the left wing root.

Cylinders of the 50-hp Coupes were exposed, but when the 65-hp version appeared in 1939, the engine (Continental) was fully cowled. Later, with the 65-hp Franklin, it became the J-4B, and the engine was again uncowled. The J-4E was fully cowled. (courtesy Ken Molson)

The Piper J-4E Coupe, powered by the 75-hp Continental engine, was introduced in April 1941, and had a cruising speed of 96 mph. A wind-driven generator and two-way radio were standard equipment. (courtesy James Borden)

Edo floats were $695, and saltwater protection was an extra $100. By 1940, a parking brake, mechanical starter, and clock were included in the standard equipment, along with an RCA radio receiver, while the price was lowered to $1,848 late that year.

Meanwhile, in March 1939, the J-4B version of the Coupe had appeared with the 60-hp Franklin engine. It was identical to the J-4A except that the engine cylinders were once again exposed. However, relatively few of this version were built, and within a year the J-4B received the 65-hp Franklin and neat, full cowling to go with it.

Early in 1940, Piper fitted a J-4 Coupe with the 65-hp Lycoming O-145 engine and designated that version the J-4F. The Lycoming O-145 got its 65 horsepower from 2550 rpm, while the Continental A-65 produced its 65 horsepower at 2300 rpm (the Franklin 4AC-176 was rated at 65 hp at 2200 rpm). An old saying among enginemen holds that there is no substitute for cubic inches. The A-65 has 171 cu. in. displacement, while the O-145 has but 144.5 cu. in., and pilots who have flown the J-3s and J-4s with both engines recall the difference in power despite the identical 65-hp ratings.

In 1941, the Cub Coupe was also offered as the J-4E with a 75-hp Continental. It was priced at $2,575. According to Juptner's *U.S. Civil Aircraft, Volume 8,* sometime in early 1941, Piper had $40,000 worth of spruce wing spars that did not pass CAA inspection, and this loss led to the use of extruded dural spars on Pipers from then on.

THE J-5 SERIES

The three-place J-5A Cub Cruiser was introduced in January 1940. Fitted with the 75-hp Continental, it was America's lowest-priced airplane with more than two seats, and it was immediately popular with small flight operators as an all-purpose machine. Dual controls allowed its use as a trainer, and the bench-type backseat, although only 37 inches wide, would accommodate two reasonably trim passengers. About 500 J-5As were sold during 1940 for $1,798 each.

Early in 1941, the Cub Cruiser was offered with the GO-145 geared Lycoming which was rated at 75 hp. This was the J-5B, and approximately 875 J-5As and Bs found new owners during 1941 and into 1942 before civil aircraft production ended for the duration of the war. Early in 1942, the J-5C, to be powered with the new 100-hp Lycoming O-235, was announced by Piper, but only 35 were built. Actually, the U.S. Navy ordered 100 variants of the J-5C, which they called the HE-1. The aft turtledeck of the HE-1 hinged upward to allow the transport of two litter patients, one above the other. The Navy later changed the designation to AE-1.

The fuselage frame was built up of welded chrome moly steel tubing as all other Pipers prior to the Comanche and Cherokee era. The Cub Cruisers had a large, single door on the right side.

The J-5C had an 18-gallon fuel tank in the right wing root, with

G.L. Brownlow of Austin, Texas with his Piper J-5 Cruiser. Brownlow had his first flying lessons in a J-4, and has since restored five Pipers. (courtesy Gail Brownlow)

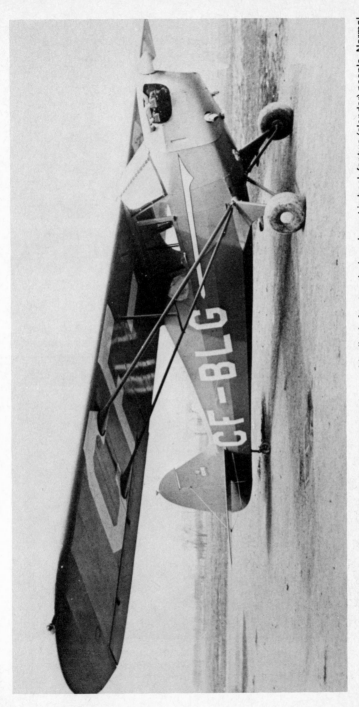

A J-5A registered in Canada. The Cub Cruisers were three-place, with pilot in front and a bench seat in back for two (slender) people. Normal cruising speed was 85 mph. (courtesy Peter M. Bowers)

A much patched J-5A registered in Mexico; September 1946. (courtesy Peter M. Bowers)

a two-gallon header tank in the fuselage. A seven-gallon or 18-gallon tank in the left wing was optional at extra cost. While other Cruisers had the J-3-type landing gear, the J-5C had its rubber shock rings in the fuselage similar to the Tri-Pacer configuration much later. The

A J-5B Cub Cruiser photographed at Kene, New Hampshire, in December 1947. The B model was fitted with the geared Lycoming engine of 75 hp. Almost 1400 J-5As and J-5Bs were produced in 1940 and 1941. (courtesy Charles Trask)

late models had a one-piece plexiglass windshield and metal wing spars.

Standard equipment on the J-5C included a wind-up mechanical engine starter, six-volt battery, position lights, hydraulic wheel brakes, steerable tailwheel, cabin heater, prop spinner, door lock, and basic flight instruments. Extra-cost items were a wind-driven generator, wheel pants, landing lights, Lear radio receiver ($63 installed!), and special paint schemes.

THE U.S. ARMY CRUISER

As war spread around the world at the beginning of the 1940s, the U.S. military, dominated by old soldiers who expected to fight the next war exactly as they fought the last one, had to be convinced that the requirements for certain weapons needed to be redefined. An example was the Army's observation airplanes, latter-day versions of the World War I deHavilland DH-4. On the eve of America's entry into World War II, Aeronca, Piper, and Taylorcraft sent loaner airplanes to the Army to demonstrate maneuvers and prove the versatility of these little craft. As a result, the North American O-47s and Curtiss O-52s—with 600 to 900 horsepower— would soon be replaced by 65-horsepower O-57 T-Crafts, O-58

The U.S. Navy purchased approximately 100 of the J-5Cs fitted with the new 100-hp Lycoming O-235-C engine, and with the turtledeck modified to swing upwards, allowing for transportation of litter patients. (courtesy of Joseph P. Juptner)

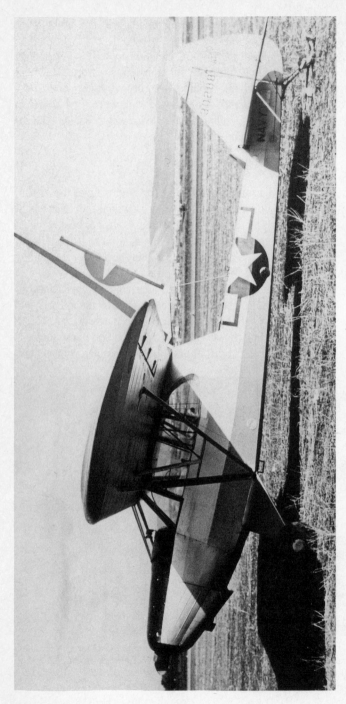

The Navy's Piper Cruiser, originally designated HE-1 and later called the AE-1, could accommodate two litter patients, one above the other, beneath the hinged turtledeck. This one was photographed on December 7, 1946. (courtesy Peter M. Bowers)

Aeroncas, and O-59 Pipers (later designated as L-2s, L-3s, and L-4s, respectively).

The many tasks performed by the little liaison airplanes during that and a couple of subsequent wars is another (proud) story. I mention them because they lead us to another, little-known, Piper.

During World War II, other liaison aircraft appeared. The Vultee L-5, with 185 hp, had no civil sister, and the L-1—originally the O-49—was a big 300-hp Stinson which also had no civil counterpart. The L-6 through L-13 were mostly prototypes, with power ranging from 65 to 600 hp. Which brings us to the L-14.

The Army ordered 850 Piper L-14s in 1945, but only five were produced before the war ended, and the remaining 845 were cancelled. These five were originally designated YL-14s, the "Y" (for service test) later dropped. Actually, the L-14, although often described as a modified J-5C, was a new design, and it received a new Approved Type Certificate, apparently in anticipation of entering the civilian market when hostilities ended. It did not. The new, immediate postwar Piper was the PA-12 Super Cruiser.

The L-14 had a large "greenhouse" that extended halfway to the vertical tail, beneath which was provision for two litter patients— one above the other—when the craft was used as an air ambulance. The L-14's most distinctive feature was its main landing gear, with

The U.S. Army ordered 850 Piper L-14s late in World War II, but the war ended before they could be produced; only five were delivered. Engine was the 125-hp O-290-C Lycoming. (courtesy Gerald Balzar)

A PA-12 Super Cruiser on Federal Skis at Keene, New Hampshire, January 20, 1948. PA-12 production began early in 1946, although its Approved Type Certificate was not issued until a year later. Engine was the 100-hp O-235-C. (courtesy Charles Trask)

a 75-inch tread and a long shock strut (anchored to the upper longeron) that utilized rubber biscuits in compression. The L-14's new 125-hp O-290-C engine, with electric starter, was fully cowled. This airplane was the first Piper with flaps, and a 14-gallon fuel tank

The Piper PA-12 Super Cruiser was priced at $3,495 "fully equipped," which included generator and radio; it cruised at 105 mph at 2350 rpm and was three-place. (courtesy Piper Aircraft Corp.)

A Piper publicity photo suggests the "good life" with a Super Cruiser. The PA-12 had an optional 19-gallon wing tank which doubled its range to 600 miles with fuel consumption of six gallons per hour. (courtesy Piper Aircraft Corp.)

was mounted in each wing, feeding to a two-gallon header tank in the usual Piper location—in the fuselage ahead of the windshield. Tires were 7.00 × 6. A wind-driven generator on the belly charged the six-volt battery. The L-14 seated two side-by-side in front, and could carry a second passenger in the rear if no litter patients were aboard.

The O-290-C installed in the L-14 was rated at 125 hp at 2,600 rpm (130 hp at 2800 rpm for takeoff). Aircraft length was 23 feet 5 inches; wingspan, 35 feet 10 inches; and height, 7 feet. Wing area was 180 sq. ft. Empty weight was 1,000 pounds; gross, 1,800 pounds; maximum speed, 115 mph; cruise, 100 mph; and stall (no flaps), 48 mph. Flaps lowered stall to 40 mph. Initial climb was 600 fpm; service ceiling, 12,000 feet; and cruising range, 300 statute miles (at 8 gph).

THE PA-12 SUPER CRUISER

Piper Aircraft Corporation resumed production of civilian airplanes in February 1946 with the three-place PA-12 Super Cruiser. Fitted with the 100-hp Lycoming O-235-C engine, the Super Cruiser was, essentially, a slicked-up version of the prewar J-5C. Normal fuel capacity was a 19-gallon tank in the right wing; a tank of equal size in the left wing was an extra-cost option. The new Super Cruiser

The Super Cruisers were normally finished in cream and Tennessee red, or yellow and light blue. A few PA-12s were built at Piper's Ponca City, Oklahoma facility, which operated briefly after World War II. (courtesy Piper Aircraft Corp.)

was certificated as Utility Category (including limited aerobatics) at 1,500 pounds gross weight, and as Normal Category at 1,750 pounds gross weight.

Almost 3,800 PA-12s were built before production ended in May 1948. A few were produced at a plant Piper had established in Ponca

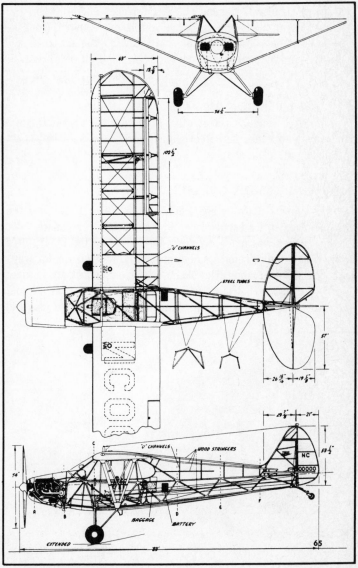

PA-12 Super Cruiser airframe.

City, Oklahoma, where the postwar Cub was in production. The Ponca City facility was closed early in 1948 after hard times overtook the U.S. general-aviation industry (from 1910 to the present, the industry has experienced recurrent cycles of boom and bust). According to Juptner's *U.S. Civil Aircraft, Volume 8*, in March 1947, Piper's main plant in Lock Haven, Pennsylvania, employed 3,000 aircraftsmen and was turning out 700 airplanes each month.

The pent-up demand for civilian lightplanes, resulting from the lack of production during the war years, saw 35,000 airplanes sold in the U.S. in 1946. But the postwar boom tapered off during the following three years. In 1947 total sales dropped to 15,617. In 1948 a total of 7,302 civilian airplanes were produced, while production went down to 3,545 in 1949.

The PA-12 Super Cruiser was of typical Piper tube-and-fabric construction—chrome moly steel in the fuselage, and dural wing spars with aluminum alloy ribs.

THE PA-14 FAMILY CRUISER

The Piper Family Cruiser, announced late in 1947, was the world's lowest priced four-place airplane-$3,825. The market for new lightplanes was markedly down by that time, and Piper, after experiencing (family) management problems, was looking for ways to mitigate the enervating sales slump—and, perhaps, simply survive. During the latter half of 1947, Piper production was almost completely suspended while a large inventory of new planes was sold

A PA-14 Family Cruiser photographed in 1949. A total of 237 of these machines were built during 14 months of production, 1948-1949. At $3,985, the Family Cruiser was the lowest-priced four-seater available. (courtesy Peter M. Bowers)

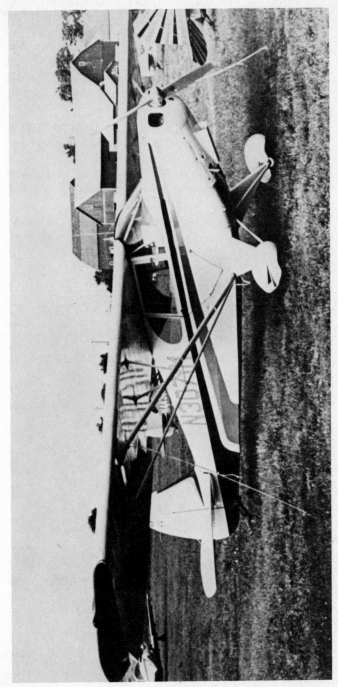

The PA-14 Family Cruiser, which entered production in April 1948, was four-place, and powered with the 108-hp Lycoming 0-235-C1. Cruising speed was 110 mph. (courtesy Joseph P. Juptner)

This PA-14 with rough-field landing gear has a 1959 Piper paint scheme. (courtesy Peter M. Bowers)

off. Meanwhile, the new PA-14 Family Cruiser was introduced to compete in the four-place field at a very low price. A new economy two-placer, the PA-15 Vagabond, appeared at the same time. Production actually began in May 1948.

Only 237 Family Cruisers were built. Compared to the PA-12, the extra seat in the Family Cruiser resulted in a cabin four inches wider, a 100-pound increase in the maximum allowable gross weight, and eight additional horsepower. The PA-12 was fitted with the 100-hp O-235-C, while the PA-14 was powered with the 108-hp O-235-C1, both rated at 2600 rpm. True, this wasn't much power for a four-place airplane, even at a modest 1,850 pounds gross weight, but minimum cost was the objective—minimum initial cost and minimum maintenance/operating costs. It's a concept whose time has come again.

The Family Cruiser was equipped with wing flaps, and standard equipment included a 12-volt electrical system with starter, position lights, and radio, plus dual stick controls, cabin heater, and basic flight instruments. The landing gear shock rings were buried inside the fuselage as on later Pipers. Production of the PA-14 sort of expired gradually, and then it was replaced altogether in mid-1949 by the PA-16 Clipper.

Piper J-4 Cub Coupe
Specifications and Performance

	J-4	J-4A
Engine	Cont A-50-1	Cont A-65
Hp and rpm.	50 @ 1900	65 @ 2300
Gross weight (lbs.).	1200	1300
Empty weight (lbs.).	710	740
Useful load (lbs.).	490	560
Wingspan (ft.).	36.12	36.12
Wing area (sq. ft.).	183	183
Length (ft.).	22.5	22.5
Height (in.).	82	82
Chord (in.).	63	63
Power loading (lbs./hp).	24	20
Wing loading (lbs./sq. ft.).	6.55	7.1
Baggage capacity (lbs.).	105	116
Fuel capacity (U.S. gal.).	16	25
Maximum speed (mph).	93	100
Cruising speed (mph).	83	92
Stalling speed (mph).	35	37
Rate of climb (initial; ft./min.).	480	600
Service ceiling (ft.).	10,500	12,000
Cruising range (statute mi.).	325	460
Fuel consumption (gal./hr.).	3.6	4.2

Piper J-4 Cub Coupe
Specifications and Performance

	J-4E	J-4F
Engine	Cont A-75	Lyc O-145
Hp and rpm	75 @ 2600	55 @ 2300
Gross weight (lbs.)	1400	1200
Empty weight (lbs.)	865	720
Useful load (lbs.)	535	480
Wingspan (ft.)	36.12	36.12
Wing area (sq. ft.)	183	183
Length (ft.)	22.5	22.5
Height (in.)	82	82
Chord (in.)	63	63
Power loading (lbs./hp)	18.66	21.8
Wing loading (lbs./sq. ft.)	6.55	6.55
Baggage capacity (lbs.)	116	105
Fuel capacity (U.S. gal.)	25	16
Maximum speed (mph)	105	95
Cruising speed (mph)	96	85
Stalling speed (mph)	40	35
Rate of climb (initial; ft./min.)	600	540
Service ceiling (ft.)	12,000	11,000
Cruising range (statute mi.)	460	340
Fuel consumption (gal./hr.)	4.9	3.8

ℓ. 1

Piper Cub Cruisers (Models J5A-75/J5B-75)
and Super Cruiser (J5C-100)
Specifications and Performance

	J-5A/J-5B	J-5C-100
Engines	Cont A-75-8	Lyc O-235-2
	Lyc GO-145	
Hp and rpm.	75 @ 2600	100 @ 2550
	75 @ 3200	
Gross weight (lbs.).	1450	1550
Empty weight (lbs.).	820	860
Useful load (lbs.).	630	890
Wingspan (ft.).	35.5	35.5
Wing area (sq. ft.).	179.3	179.3
Length (ft.).	22.5	22.5
Height (in.).	82	82
Propeller diameter (max. in.).	74	74
Power loading (lbs./hp).	19.3	15.5
Wing loading (lbs./sq. ft.).	8.09	8.64
Baggage capacity (lbs.).	41	41
Fuel capacity (U.S. gal.).	25	20
Tire size.	8.00 × 4	8.00 × 4
Maximum speed (mph).	95	110
Cruising (mph @ 3,000 ft.).	80	95
Stalling speed (mph).	43	45
Rate of climb (initial; ft./min.).	400	650
Service ceiling (ft.).	13,000	16,000
Cruising range (statute mi.).	380	238*

*With 38 gal. optional tanks, 431 mi.

Piper Super Cruiser (PA-12)
and Family Cruiser (PA-14)
Specifications and Performance

	PA-12	PA-14
Engine	Lyc O-235	Lyc O-235-C1
Hp and rpm	100 @ 2600	115 @ 2800
Gross weight (lbs.)	1750*	1850*
Empty weight (lbs.)	950	1020
Wingspan (ft.)	35.5	35.5
Wing area (sq. ft.)	179.3	179.3
Length (ft.)	22.8	23.25
Height (in.)	82	77
Propeller diameter (max. in.)	76	74
Power loading (lbs./hp)	17.5	17.1
Wing loading (lbs./sq. ft.)	9.8	10.3
Baggage capacity (lbs.)	41	80
Fuel capacity (U.S. gal.)	38	38
Tire pressure (lbs./sq. in.)	18	22
Maximum speed (mph)	114	123
Cruise (mph)	105	110
Stalling speed (mph)	42	46**
Rate of climb (initial; ft./min.)	600	600
Service ceiling (ft.)	12,600	12,500
Absolute ceiling (ft.)	15,500	14,500
Cruising range (statute mi.)	600	500
Fuel consumption (gal./hr.)	6.5	7

*1500 and 1550 lbs. respectively in utility category.

**With flaps.

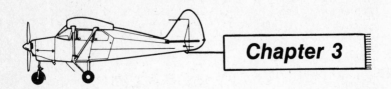

Chapter 3

The Vagabonds

The PA-15 and PA-17 Piper Vagabonds were introduced in mid-1948 less than a month apart, although the prototype had flown the previous October. About 500 of the PA-15 version and over 200 of the PA-17 model were built through 1950, when production ended.

THE PA-15

The PA-15 was the economy model. It contained almost nothing that did not directly contribute to sustained, manned flight. It was a two-placer with side-by-side seating, but had flight controls on the left only. It had no floor mat, no shock absorbers (its Goodyear doughnut tires did the shock absorbing), no engine primer, no cabin heat, and was powered with the Lycoming O-145 of 65 alleged horsepower. But the PA-15 Vag did have brakes, and the anemic Lyc was so well muffled that the lack of soundproofing in the cabin was hardly noticed. Its cabin was roomy and its windshield large. It employed the standard Cub wing, with three feet cut from the root of each panel. The PA-15 was priced, fly-away-factory, at $1,995.

This airplane was manufactured with both spruce and dural wing spars. The 12-gallon fuel tank was mounted ahead of the windshield.

The Piper PA-17 Vagabond, photographed at the EAA Oshkosh Fly-In/Convention, owned by Keith Swalheim of Stoughton, Wisconsin. (courtesy Don Downie)

THE PA-17

The PA-17 Vagabond was fitted with the A-65 Continental engine and, priced at about $200 more than the PA-15, was equipped with most of the amenities its plain-Jane sister lacked. Standard equipment included dual controls, floor mat, shock absorbers, flight instruments/engine gauges, and propeller spinner. Extra-cost options included wheel pants, radio, McCauley metal propeller, landing lights, and a six-gallon auxiliary fuel tank in the left wing root.

Many Vagabonds flying today have been given larger engines, but I have always believed that a Vag powered with a 65-hp Continental offered the best combination of economy and performance. If you fly from mountain airstrips, more power is desirable, especially on warm days, but for us "flatlanders" she's a nice little fun airplane just the way David Long designed her.

PIPER PEOPLE

Mention of Dave Long suggests that we should take a quick look at the people who made things go at Piper Aircraft during the days when the Piper Classics were designed and built.

William Thomas Piper, Sr.—President and Board Chairman of Piper Aircraft Corporation throughout the period of the fabric-covered machines. Born in Knapps Creek, NY, on January 8, 1881,

Science teacher Sarah Kaeiser of Lake City, Florida with her PA-17 Vagabond. Sarah flew her Vag to Menomonie, Wisconsin, for a workshop on her first out-of-state cross-country. (courtesy Sarah Kaeiser)

attended Harvard University, and worked as a construction engineer for U.S. Steel Corp., 1903-1916. With partner Ralph Lloyd, developed oil field holdings in the Bradford, Pennsylvania area, 1914-1929. Invested in Taylor Brothers Aircraft in 1928 (as related in the Introduction). Died in 1970 at the age of 89; however, control of the company he founded had passed to other investors during the 1960s. (At publication time, Piper had been recently purchased by M. Stuart Millar).

William Thomas Piper, Jr.—Executive Vice President in 1955, and "connected" with Piper from 1934. Born September 8, 1911 in Sharpsburg, Pennsylvania; B.A. from Harvard.

Thomas Francis Piper—Vice President, Operations. Born August 13, 1914; B.S. from Harvard. USAAF pilot, 1942-1946.

Howard "Pug" Piper—Vice President, Research and Development; born in Bradford, Pennsylvania, November 3, 1917. Attended Harvard; joined his father at Piper in 1939; served as Naval Aviator, 1942-1945. Returned to Piper Aircraft in 1945; executive vice president, 1950-1968. Worked for Beech, 1968-1973. Was a free-lance consultant until death in April 1981.

Walter Corey Jamouneau—Vice President, Engineering 1937-1969. Previously Chief Engineer of Taylor Brothers Aircraft (J-2 and first J-3s), 1933-1937. (The "J" in the designations of the J-2 through J-5 was for "Jamouneau.") Born in Irvington, New Jersey, September 21, 1912; B.S. from Rutgers; multiengine pilot rating.

VAGABOND ADVENTURES

The following stories were written by Steve Ogles of Coronado, California, for the *Vagabond News,* a publication devoted to the activities of Piper Vagabond owners. Steve's Vagabond has a C-85 Continental engine and a 60-amp alternator.

To the West Indies in a Vagabond

When you finish something that you have spent a good deal of time, money, and energy on (and a little bit of someone else's time and money), you quite naturally want to do something to reward yourself, and in some way include your project. So it is that N4696H, with an engine retrofit and assorted goodies, and a pilot with an eye for distant places, take to the air for a flight—on summer wings.

For some time I had had my eye on a round trip to Puerto Rico. I just happen to love the ocean, being an avid waterman and having

The PA-15 Vagabond was fitted with the 65-hp O-145 Lycoming. Priced at $1,990, the PA-15 preceded the PA-17 by only a month or so in mid-1948. (courtesy Peter M. Bowers)

lived by it my entire life. Flying to distant places is pretty much a novelty in itself. When you can fly to a place and enjoy the sun, beaches, and tropical clear waters, and even have that place be outside the continental United States, well, that can be even more pleasurable. We join our flight now in the hangar at Hemet Ryan Field in the final hours before embarking.

I finish up my wingtip strobe installation (I was told by a fellow pilot one night that the strobes make the Vagabond look as if it were moving at 200 knots), and start to load the airplane.

The void under the seats and just behind provide ample space for: one four-foot Morey Surfrider; two full-sized pillows; masks, fins, snorkels, and wetsuits for two; two bedroll mats; plus assorted life support systems. With the seat bar back in place, we fill the baggage compartment to the limit which, incidentally, comes to considerably more than 401 pounds. Between the seats (I have buckets), we find room for flashlight, rags, oil funnel, cookies, etc. At the flight deck there is room for me, the 170-pound pilot-in-command, and Mike, 120-pound passenger-in-command. Mike is 18 and has never been too far from home; a non-pilot, but dedicated waterman and friend— and, yes, he has half the cash for gas.

"Four Six Niner Six Hotel off the ground at zero, four, four, five," I broadcast on Unicom like an airliner confirming time off with his dispatcher. Surely, there in the Los Angeles Basin someone hears this historic flight heading out to somewhere. Searching out over the mountains, we pick up our eastbound heading. I've this notion to try my best to make Ozona, Texas, the day's terminating point.

Oil temperature up a bit; a sure sign of the sun. Times are good now; there are only two PSA DC-10s hugging dry shelter under the sun on the ramp at Marana, Arizona. Back in '73 I remember row upon row of 707s, DC-8s, and others as the recession took its toll.

At Marana the engine is introduced to its first dose of LL100. It is not to be the last, as 80 octane will be found at only a few places.

Quickly back into the air so as to beat the desert heat, we proceed on toward Tucson. The military jets in the pattern there almost push us into the mountains. Perhaps they are just curious about this little airplane, or maybe they are using us for a target. Boy, if they only knew who they are tangling with—we can open up on them with peanut butter and squirts of apple juice.

As we near Sunland, Texas, I tune to 122.0, and a Falcon Jet somewhere in the stratosphere recites winds aloft to El Paso Flight Watch and asks for weather at Las Vegas. Hmmmmmmm, I thought Flight Watch was for kids like me at 10,000 feet and below.

All is well until we reach a point about 20 miles out, inbound. A monster thunderstorm, which we can clearly see, is near Sunland. Flight Watch asks me what the picture looks like from my viewpoint. "Well, sir, it's rip-roaring to the north and ahead, while mellow, mellow to the south and behind."

Flight Watch stays with us until we are five miles out ("Thanks, pardner"). Cattails at the approach end of the runway yield to the wind. We slide overhead and are stopped at the numbers. A lineman beckons us to expedite to a tiedown directly in front of the pumps. Filled with 24 gallons of green gas, Mike and I make haste to keep our wings firm on Texas soil as the storm moves in.

It is 3:30 P.M. before we are airborne again. We're so close to the Mexican border that Mike enjoyed tacos and a bullfight, while on the other half of the plane I kept an ear to El Paso Approach Control and sadly contemplated the tail end of a peanut butter sandwich.

Somewhere between airport symbols on the Sectional chart across my lap it happens. After a day-long session of beef jerky, cheese crackers, oatmeal cookies, candy, and warm apple juice, Mike looks green. He takes refuge in an American Airlines "discomfort bag."

Shortly, we begin to pick up foul headwinds ripping across the Texas plains. The resulting dust storm occasionally takes the ground from our view, along with a town or two. The dust cloud rises to our cruising altitude, and the Vagabond's fat tires roll across the top. On we go. Crazy winds, a stop at Fort Stockton for fuel, and we continue eastbound, the sun completing its zillionth trek across the sky. Compass heading is abandoned as the wind takes its toll.

Then, in darkness, we continue smoothly over headlights on the highway. A light rain under a Texas sky, and passenger-in-command

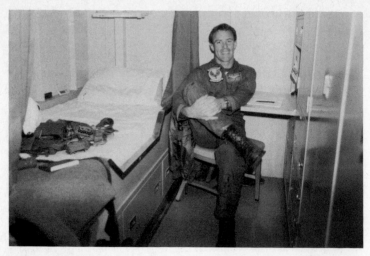

U.S. Navy carrier pilot Steven Ogles in his quarters aboard ship. Steven flew his 85-hp Vagabond round-trip to the West Indies from his home in Coronado, California. Steven's adventure is described in this chapter. (courtesy Steven Ogles)

has journeyed to a silent world of dreams. Half an hour goes by, and it's Niner Six Hotel on final at Ozona. There is heavy, summer night baseball action off the approach end of the runway on two fields. The crowds look up to our magnificent set of wings.

As the time of night would have it, the airport is deserted. That's just perfect. We secure the airplane on the grass right in front of the terminal shack. Mike and I check the Sectionals for our next day's flight. A car wheels up, windows all rolled down. Happy faces with hot dogs stuffed in them give wide-eyed looks of curiosity, then disappear. No tiedown fees here, no bother, no nothing. Ozona will always be home for an eve on these transcontinental excursions, a Vagabond pilot's place. We catch some sleep after the satisfying reminder that 11.8 hours in the air netted nearly 1,000 miles in spite of rain, winds, and darkness. We did it!

The dream of a coast-to-coast flight in two days is deflated on the following day as eastbound progress increasingly leads into poor weather.

We meet a real nice guy out in the Mississippi wilderness. We land with less than an hour's fuel left, and wouldn't you know, I pick this one for a fuel stop and there's no fuel. All is not lost, because it happens to be a skydiver training day out there on the bayou, and the jumpmaster just happens to have a 55-gallon drum of avgas on a trailer. This guy must have seen me coming all the way from California. Mike pumps about a half-gallon, and the guy yells for him to stop. "That's all I can spare," he says, sticking my fiver into his pocket. "That's my price, son."

Airborne, I throttle us into the most economical power setting, bee-lining for Tyler Municipal, where a friendly radar controller brings us all the way down to final approach amongst thick rain cells and accompanying weather phenomena—some kind of service for a slow old airplane with no transponder.

Fueled and questioned—and even a "Hey, I used to own one of those little buggers!"—we're ready to press on. Luckily, the radar man who led us in by the nose, leads us out the same way. He more than makes up for the bandit in the bayou.

Lightning flashes on Mike's side of the airplane as we rollercoaster out of the turbulence . . . soon we're in smooth air, under an overcast in drizzle, which dictates landings at various "uninhabited" airports. Upon landing where we think we can call a Flight Service Station, we find ourselves viewing a phone booth blasted by a shotgun and inhabited with wasps. An old Cessna 210 is identified as having been seized by the sheriff. Deciding this is a loser for the night, we flee the place after a couple of hours and a supper of oatmeal cookies.

Half an hour later it's over for the day; surrounded by trees, it's out here in the boonies engulfed by that steamy, after-rain silence. Mosquitoes rise in direct proportion to our skin temperatures.

Morning finds two weary ("smelling good") bodies sitting by the airplane, faces pointed skyward toward the sun's presumed position. We finally see the sawmill's tower.

By mid-afternoon we're in radar contact and on the ground at Jacksonville, Florida. Mike has a friend there, so we part company for a few days. I fly over to Waycross, Georgia, to stay with the Garrett family, the family that treated me so well on my first venture to the East Coast. A shower, clean hair, and air conditioning make one feel real again . . .

I depart Waycross for Jacksonville International and call Approach at 10. They tell me to report five miles, and to expect vectors to Runway Niner. They understand that I'm a negative squawker.

"Niner Six Hotel is five miles."

"Niner Six Hotel, descend to and maintain two thousand on two-two-zero heading. Call when airport is in sight."

Minutes pass. "Jax, Niner Six Hotel does not have field in sight."

Then, from out of the blue (literally): "Jax Approach, Eastern Two Six Niner. We got the little guy in sight and he is just about there."

"Thanks, Eastern!" The pulp mill smoke has a break right at the edge of Runway Nine. "Niner Six Hotel; airport in sight."

So goes it; still air, stinky smoke, and a two-mile stretch that is Runway Nine. A man in an orange shirt uses our Vagabond to fill a small space between a T-tailed King Air and a Learjet (is this guy laughing?). I close the thrust lever, the engines spool down, and the faint smell of kerosene fills the air. The electric gyros whir as I check the digital readouts—and the dream fades. I tell the guy I'll take on 60 pounds of 100 octane, and smile. Mike says to hurry—"I'm about to choke on this foul air."

Pulp smoke fills our cabin as I click the proper frequencies and our wings speed away from the ground. Niner Six Hotel is airborne again, with friend, and southbound. Our destination lay beyond . . . the myths of the Bermuda Triangle.

There's a series of small rain storms along the way to Ft. Pierce, Florida, and VFR traffic abounds. We have to get clearance through every control zone along the Atlantic down the Florida coast.

At Ft. Pierce we swing our compass, the only reason for our stop. After all, as eastern migration produces a compass error of 20 to 25 degrees, it can only be considered in the best interest of all concerned to take corrective action. Mike wanders off in the final moments of the compass swing and I find him devouring a burger and fries in the airport restaurant—"Just having my last meal." Some confidence.

We pick a runway and blast off for Tilford's at West Palm Beach. Tilford's gen-av terminal is utopia; they've got it all. The humor here is the same as elsewhere when I point to the Vagabond and to the destination on my Caribbean WAC charts. I get a weather briefing and file our flight plan.

The Bahamas

As I talk with Departure Control, our wings feel a tad heavy with our extra cargo of five quarts of oil and four gallons of water on the floorboard—not to mention two large jars of Buddy Boy peanut butter and eight loaves of bread tied to a string drifting along in the aft fuselage. At 6500 feet, we are in level, loaded cruise tracking nicely on course. Water blows along smoothly in our favor, turning aqua-emerald green from deep blue hues. I'm definitely one of those who have no qualms about flying over any kind of water.

Westend, Grand Bahama Island, beckons us from 20 miles in the distance. The extra-cool controller in the tower gives us a clear-to-land in a thick chocolate accent. Customs? Sooo easy in and out. After that we fly on over to Freeport (same island), get some fuel, and do a short map ritual on the ramp there.

That map ritual was the beginning of some of the most beautiful, pleasant, and exciting flying I've encountered. We covered every island in the Bahama chain, and went even farther to the Turks and Caicos Islands, British West Indies. Diving was, of course, spectacular—as were the people and some of the local foods Mike and I sampled.

Much of our flight down through the islands was against a prevailing 30-knot wind. That, and some heavy thunderstorm action, were reasons for concern on more than one occasion. One hundred octane fuel was always available; the only critical fuel situation was a four-and-a-half-hour leg from Georgetown, Great Exuma Island, Bahamas, to South Caicos Island, Turks, and Caicos Islands, British West Indies. We had, perhaps, a 30-minute reserve when we landed—not bad—but not real good considering the flying we were doing.

The longest over-water leg I attempted was a 270-mile stretch between Georgetown, Great Exuma, and Westend, Grand Bahama Island, on our way back up through the islands. If my description of this portion of my venture seems vague and lacking in detail, I'm truly sorry, but this part of the adventure was something you had to see for yourself, you just had to be there. Written descriptions simply cannot do it justice.

The Long Way Home

Entering Customs back into the States is simple, except for the $25 overtime charge for arrivals after five o'clock. The inspector at West Palm is more than sympathetic, however, and knows we are on a budget flight.

Departing West Palm, we press onward, contacting Jacksonville

A PA-17 Vagabond at Oshkosh in 1972. The PA-17 was powered with the A-65 Continental engine and was equipped with shocks, floor mat, and other basics that its plain-Jane sister did not have. (courtesy Charles Trask)

Approach Control 45 minutes after sunset. The controller asks if we'd like sequence lights. Why not? This night approach is probably the most fantastically colorful I'll ever witness from the Vagabond.

Jacksonville marks the end of the odyssey for Mike. He will spend a few weeks with his friend here, then streak home in a silver tube. He was a good passenger-in-command—light, good humor, and always knew when it was his turn to pay for fuel.

My next whim takes me north, through the eastern seaboard states: flying in smoky haze that goes from ground level to 11,000 feet, with no visual ground contact; a man in a white shirt and tie nearly pulling his hair out at the sight of me hand-propping at Savannah, Georgia; taking off behind a Viscount which was taking off behind a flight of jet fighters; sitting through a laser-light electrical storm during the nighttime hours at Williamsburg, Virginia; and watching my sneakers sail along in one of those funny little rivers that form in a hard rain (I found them the next morning). Finally I reach my favorite stop on the East Coast: Ansonia, Connecticut, just a little way in from the coast, and home of the Vagabonds East and Jimmie Jenkins. Jim is a long-standing Vagabond friend. Flying the New England states in the summer is beautiful—soft green and rolling hills. The air is very clear.

Jim and I are going to fly formation to Oshkosh . . . but his engine fails and there is no way to have it fixed in time to leave. Plans for him to go along with me in Niner-Six-Hotel are also shot down by forces beyond our control. So, with a clean airplane and a fresh oil change—the first since leaving California—I wing it alone for Oshkosh.

Once again, my primary concern is weather—rain and low clouds. I manage to make it into the airport adjacent to Kent State University in Ohio just as the ceiling and night close in. I secure the airplane right at the gas pumps and spend the night taking pictures and hoping for sunshine the following morning.

The weather in the morning is lousy but flyable. Gradually, I am able to get up around 5,000 feet, and no sooner do I get there than the ground below disappears. I spiral down through a hole over a railroad track and find that, at 200 feet, I can make super time. There are no radio/TV towers or anything as such, just a clean shot into Norwalk, Ohio. At Norwalk there are a few others bound for Oshkosh, but there isn't any fuel, and I need some badly—especially flying in rather marginal conditions.

Pressing on, I find fuel, and cross the VOR at Kalamazoo. Cruising at 10,500 just a few minutes out from the VOR, a big, black bee creams himself in a head-on with my Vagabond, then spins earthward.

The direct route is for me, so I set out a straight course from South Haven, Michigan, some 120 miles over Lake Michigan to Oshkosh. I make it into Oshkosh with no time to spare before they close the field for the airshow.

I spend three days wandering around at Oshkosh with my parents and, as usual, leave on a Wednesday in poor weather. Shortly after my departure, listening to various frequencies, I hear hair-raising tales of pilots encountering golf-ball-sized hail; but soon enough the bad weather is behind and I eventually follow one of those large transmission-line trails into the sunset and a smooth touchdown at Clarinda, Iowa, for an evening of unbearable heat.

At 1:00 A.M., huge raindrops play a steady rhythm on Niner Six Hotel's drum-tight Dacron skin. The morning looks bad and is. I fly a 250-mile divert to the north to get around an awesome weather front. In the Midwest, cornfields and foul winds are forever—at least on the days I fly through. The evening gets me to Tucumcari, New Mexico, 30 minutes after sunset.

I wonder if it ever cooled off in Tucumcari? I'm sure it cooled to at least 90° the night I slept there. The heat was so oppressive I made a 4:00 A.M. departure with the coyotes howling.

The ground below became familiar once again. Deming, New Mexico, to Gila Bend, Arizona (a story in itself!), then to Hemet-Ryan, home for Vagabond Niner Six Hotel. As for me, I still had to drive another 80 miles south to Coronado, home for me.

Steven Ogles Surfs the Baja with a Vagabond

In two quasi-official offices, near the base of the control tower, papers were checked in proper order, stamped, and signed. Crossing the border went smoothly this morning. The boys in the radar room at San Diego TRACON were probably still wondering who it was that so carefully snuck around the new Terminal Control Area.

The Immigration and Flight Plan offices were small, drab, and familiar. The teletype was silent behind the counter, but there was a note on the chalkboard informing that some excavation was being done adjacent to the runway at Loreto.

There's never much waiting around or confusion when I come through here. Of course, being the first flight across the border on a weekday should have some reward. Although I've been through the motions here a dozen or so times, each border crossing still leaves a standing impression lingering within. Baja holds a repeated sense of adventure as each new trip begins.

Memories surface, bringing tattletale recollections of past excursions. The feeling, like that of surfing and flying, will never exit my soul or become old and jaded with time or repetition. Surfing by airplane is an experience that lends itself uniquely to the Baja Peninsula. My Vagabond is a good one. Its soft clean lines reflect the design of the time—short, fat, and rounded, perched atop thick, pudgy tires.

A PA-15 seen at Wenatchee, Washington in 1953. Approximately 500 were produced from 1948 through 1950. (courtesy Peter M. Bowers)

Sometimes a Mexican fuel truck is just about as hard to locate as empty surf. When you do find the truck, the hide-and-seek anguish will quickly evaporate. Avgas 80/87 squirts from the truck to your empty tanks for 75 cents per gallon. Arabian liquid gold, north of the border, trickles into your thirsty machine for about $1.60 per gallon. The Pemex price is twice as nice.

Let's see, tanks are full and I've got my Flight Plan and General Declaration. It's time to get started down the southbound airway. "Tijuana Tower, Niner Six Hotel is currently outbound the two-one-zero-degree radial, climbing through six thousand feet, ten miles south. Clear your Control Zone."

"Roger, ah, Niner Six Hotel, ah, frequency change approved, and, ah, have a nice flight."

"Niner Six Hotel. Thank you." And a few minutes later, climbing in a loaded cruise, taped music replaces the controller's voice en route to the air-conditioned state of 9500 feet and 100 miles per hour. That south-of-the-border feeling soon settles in. Everything I've managed to pack into my small airplane is now like water in the desert.

By late morning a fuel stop is taken. Gasoline is pumped from 55-gallon drums in the back of a pickup truck, and I hand out packs of cigarettes as gratuities.

"Hace calor," exclaims Llano.

"It sure is hot, you old Mexican," I agree. "Feels good, though; I like this dry heat."

"Adonde va?" he queries.

"Voy a Cabo San Lucas para las holas," I reply, pointing to my surfboard.

"Ah, muy bien. Va solo?" he inquires.

"Yeah, I'm always alone; story of my life. Adios, see you in a few weeks on my way back."

On takeoff out of Santa Inez I lose an unopened bag of M&Ms out the window. My old flight instructor always warned, "Never leave anything on the instrument panel during takeoff unless you want to lose it."

With that unpleasant moment in the past, the view outside the plane begins to absorb my attention. Below my wings a scorching Baja melts into a diamond-textured ocean of cracked emerald . . . the Pacific and Gulf Coasts can be seen with a single panoramic scan. Nearly two miles below me, that black ribbon, which is symbolic of automobile driving endurance, winds over the torrid terrain, but there is no sign of a car in either direction.

It is slightly less than four hours to my next stop, and the view from the airplane, matched with good music, suspends time from my consciousness—well, almost.

On the tattered pavement under a brassy sun at Loreto, much attention is directed at my wooden propeller as I hurriedly file another "Plan de Vuelo."

"Tu quieres dos tankos con gasolina ochenta, todo?"

"Yeah. Fill 'er up."

Inside the huge, palm-thatched airport office my orderly collection of papers does nothing to speed the Airport Commandante as his fingers hunt-and-peck across the keyboard. His vintage Smith-Corona reeks from an overzealous dose of lubricant.

"Ah, va a Cabo San Lucas," he notes.

"Yes, that is where I'm headed," I confirm.

"Bueno." He sighs. "Combustible a bordo?"

"Gas, ah, six hours; yeah, six."

"Bueno, es todo," he mutters. "Adios."

The western sky warms my face against the coolness aloft. Sunset should be around eight o'clock this evening. Computations on my E6B computer estimate completion of this last leg of my flight in about 2.7 hours. It looks pretty good. I've got enough fuel to fly twice that far.

It doesn't last—the euphoria, that is. The sky ahead and to the west begins to look ominous. Thinking ahead, I know I'm going to have to take some action before long. And by the time I cross the Omni station over La Paz International, the sky has become more than I can handle. Towering cumulus clouds are in all quadrants, their tops rifling straight up through the troposphere. From experience, I know that any time I go the distance, it will be one thing or another. Along the base of the storm, shafts of lightning vein jaggedly downward, illuminating the torrential downpour.

61

This PA-17 Vag was photographed at Oshkosh in 1973. Only 200 PA-17s were produced, although they were priced only $200 above the PA-15. (courtesy Charles Trask)

The only way to Cabo now is to lose about 9000 feet of altitude and make a run at some low-level contour flying.

I'm hugging the ground along the eastern side of the Sierra San Lorenzo mountains as the brilliant daylight gradually erodes into a disconcerting grey. The first smattering drops of rain strip the bugs from the windscreen before settling into a swirling aerodynamic ballet. A dull hum fills the cabin as my rain-streaked wings meet the storm. I turn up the cockpit light and flood the instrument panel in iridescent red.

Coming up over Costa Azul, I can see a few four-foot waves racing along the beach. Not a soul is in the rain-splattered water. Just a few more minutes farther south and my destination is visible. I'll be in the water 20 minutes later, my tent erect on the beach next to a palapa, and my airplane parked in the usual spot. All of this under a warm sky that is about to break open again with sunshine. It's times like this when I wonder why I ever surf at home.

My friend Jim Montalbano and his girlfriend Teresa arrive late the next night. It seems that their attempts to catch an air taxi out of La Paz were foiled by leaky hydraulics and the pilot's lament, "De plane, she is no good." And that after a five-hour layover at the airport.

Now I know what this kind of thing can do to Jim. It is only a mild surprise to me when he wheels up to the beach in a taxicab. "Heck," he shrugs, "It only cost me sixty dollars."

"Surfers are an affluent bunch," I said.

This isn't the first time Jim and I have surfed in this area . . . a good feature is that the main road is within easy reach, providing a link with civilization and a route to good rock climbing. You don't go to the east Cape just to surf.

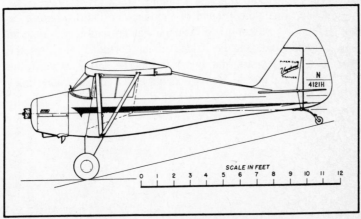

A side-view drawing of the Vagabond. (courtesy James Triggs)

An entire cast of creatures hides on the beaches and in the waters along the east Cape. And there are just as many nocturnal devils as daytime ones. The late-night crab rodeo with "Whitey Dog" will forever be my favorite after-dark sporting event. You've never seen a dog dig for crabs, then tear 'em apart the way Whitey Dog does. Man, it's wild!

From the air, the coastline along the east Cape leads your attention from one point to the next. Each point looks custom-made for surfing. North of San Jose del Cabo, the first in a series of three shipwrecks appears, tuna seiners of a tide long since gone to sea. Each rusting hulk marks a potential for excellent surf, a marker for those who stray beyond the beaten path. Everywhere you look there is another spot, another point. You can't help but recall the stories and pictures that come out of this place.

Sitting in the shade one afternoon, I picture the armchair surfer. At home, he stops the gap easily. He reaches back for something cool from a well-stocked icebox, thumbs through a surf magazine. His thoughts linger on the evening's party, his well-styled "surf looks," and the radiant chrome on his (never been) off-road four-wheel drive.

The surfer hides in the scarce shade of a few palm fronds, drinking 100-degree water, scratching the bites, and keeping the bugs from his ears and nose. He views the peanut butter and jelly sandwich with equanimity, pondering the jelly jar and wondering how long the ants will survive the thick morass of grape.

Steven Ogles is a U.S. Navy carrier pilot and a modest young man. However, I can report that Steven purchased his Vagabond from San Diego Auto Body as a runout wreck for $350.

Steven began the rebuild of this airplane shortly before he completed the seventh grade. The job was finished by the time he was 16 years old, and he soloed on his birthday. He flew the Vagabond for 11 years, during which time he flew it twice to the West Indies, and up and down Mexico's Baja Peninsula more times than he could recall.

Piper Vagabonds (PA-15 and PA-17)
Specifications and Performance

	PA-15	PA-17
Engine	Lyc O-145	Cont A-65
Hp and rpm	65 @ 2550	65 @ 2300
Gross weight (lbs.)	1100	1150
Empty weight (lbs.)	630	650
Wingspan (ft.)	29.3	29.3
Wing area (sq. ft.)	147.5	147.5
Length (ft.)	18.7	18.7
Height (in.)	72	72
Propeller diameter (in.)	72	72
Power loading (lbs./hp)	16.8	17.7
Wing loading (lbs./sq. ft.)	7.5	7.8
Baggage capacity (lbs.)	40	40
Fuel capacity (U.S. gal.)	12	12
Maximum speed (mph)	100	100
Cruising speed (mph)	90	90
Stalling speed (mph)	45	45
Rate of climb (initial; ft./min.)	510	530
Service ceiling (ft.)	10,000	10,500
Cruising range (statute mi.)	250	250
Tread (in.)	69	69
Interior cabin width (in.)	39	39

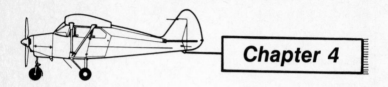

Chapter 4

The Clipper and Pacer

The PA-16 Clipper appeared concurrent with the new PA-18 Super Cub early in 1949. The Clipper was, essentially, a four-place version of the Vagabonds; its empty weight was only 200 pounds more, but it had almost twice the power. Whether or not it was so intended, the Clipper was an interim machine, and only 726 were produced before the PA-20 Pacer took its market late in 1949.

THE PA-16 CLIPPER

The Clipper's engine was the 115-hp Lycoming O-235-C1. Fuel, of course, was 80/87-octane avgas, and the compression ratio was 6.75:1. The Clipper's propeller was the Sensenich 73FM-52.

The PA-16 had poor brakes and a landing gear tread that could have been a bit wider. As it was, you had to pay attention on landing rollout to prevent a ground loop in any kind of a crosswind. Like all other Pipers of its generation, its flight characteristics were gentle and predictable, and any flying machine that comes close to delivering one mile per hour for each horsepower has got to be considered efficient. With full tanks (36 gallons), the Clipper could carry 600 pounds of people and baggage, or only 75 pounds less than the 150-hp Piper Cherokee Cruiser 15 years later. Clearly, a little more power and a few other small changes would result in a truly nice little four-seater.

THE PA-20 PACER

A truly nice little four-seater was the PA-20 Pacer, deliveries of which began late in 1949 (1950 model). A total of 1,119 Pacers were built before production ended in 1952. The first ones were offered with the 115-hp O-235 engine, but the optional 125-hp O-290-D was fitted to most, and was considered the standard powerplant for the Pacer after the first month or so of production. An option on later models was the 135-hp O-290-D2, along with an Aeromatic propeller.

The Aeromatic has been described as a "poor boy's" constant-speed propeller—well, not exactly "constant-speed." The counterbalance weights on the hub allow high rpm and low blade pitch for takeoff, and an increased blade pitch for cruise. The cruise setting may be changed on the ground by changing the counterbalance weights. Univair owns the type certificate for the Aeromatic propeller, which is also found on some Piper Cruisers, Family Cruisers, and Clippers, originally factory-installed as an extra-cost option. (Univair is supposed to have purchased Piper's inventory of components for the fabric-covered machines, but Wag-Aero also stocks some original Piper parts.)

Lila Johnson with her PA-20 Pacer. Husband Clay Johnson was a flight operator and Piper dealer at the Lawton (Oklahoma) Municipal Airport during the 1950s and early '60s. The above machine was powered by the 125-hp Lycoming O-290-D engine. (courtesy Lila Johnson)

The Pacer is equipped with flaps, front and rear doors, a pair of 18-gallon wing tanks, and a removable rear seat for cargo hauling. I have been told by a current Pacer owner that the last ones, the 1952 models, had a wider-tread landing gear than the earlier ones, but I have not been able to confirm that. My personal experience with Pacers was limited—right seat—and a long time ago.

Many Pacer owners have re-engined with the 150-hp O-320 Lycoming, which is supposed to result in a 1,000-pound empty weight with a 2,000-pound gross. That may be pushing things a little. The Tri-Pacer with 150 hp has an empty weight of 1,100 pounds and a gross weight of 2,000 pounds. And while we're on the subject, a lot of Tri-Pacers have been converted to tailwheel configuration. You might check with Univair, Wag-Aero, or the Short Wing Piper Club for Supplemental Type Certificates.

A recent issue of *Trade-A-Plane* listed only two Pacers for sale, both 135 hp. Prices were $12,500 and $7,900—sounds like one very neat plane, and one needing a lot of work. Another means of locating a used fabric-covered Piper is by way of an aircraft-wanted ad in the *Short Wing Piper News* (see appendix for the address).

Pacer Ownership

The following are excerpts from a report on Piper Pacer ownership by Bill Kleinbauer, which originally appeared in the November/December 1985 issue of the *Short Wing Piper News*.

In August, 1983, I visited my friend Dave Cooper. Dave was hanging from the hospital ceiling in traction after spending four days in intensive care following a serious motorcycle accident. I asked him what I could do to help, and he said, "Sell my airplane." He was not going to be physically able to fly it for about two years, and he could use the money to buy a new car with an automatic transmission.

I went to the Torrance (California) Airport and got checked out in his Pacer taildragger so that I could demonstrate it to prospective buyers. This PA-20, Seven Seven Two Six Kilo, was ratty—rotted headliner, rusted areas, low compression on #4 cylinder, crazed windshield, shimmying tailwheel on some landings, old 90-channel nav/com, and old instruments—strictly VFR capability. But it was tied down at G&S Industries, and maintained in almost acceptable flying condition by G&S's owner, Bob Hamilton, who maintains Bob Hoover's P-51, so I felt that he could keep Two Six Kilo operating okay.

Dave wanted $6,500 for the airplane, but in a weak moment said he would consider taking $5,000, since one cylinder might have to be replaced (it did).

One evening, after a good dinner and wine at Cafe Pierre in Manhattan Beach, I went to the pay phone, called Dave, and said I'd buy his airplane for $5,000. He agreed.

I had been flying on and off since 1957, and had 650 hours of flying adventures.

What I want to do now is give the Short Wing Piper Club members a summary of my experiences for the last two years in making Pacer Two Six Kilo the satisfying machine it is today, both for IFR and VFR use.

Tailwheels

My Maule tailwheel shimmied badly on about one out of five landings. I changed to the Scott 3200 tailwheel, and still got a shimmy once in a while. The swivel plate was changed to make it horizontal (as specified) rather than tilted forward, and I went to the Scott tailwheel control springs in place of the Maule springs. The shimmy is gone. One item of caution: For a short time, I did use the Maule compression-style tailwheel springs and when shimmy occurred, the springs bottomed out and bent the tailwheel control arms mounted on the bottom of the rudder—although the aluminum for the control arms may have been in a soft condition due to a welding repair to the part after the shaft broke from previous shimmys.

Jensen Wing Strut Fittings

After getting educated about the strength problems with the wing-strut fork fittings, I decided to have double-the-diameter Jensen fittings installed. Orion Air, at the San Luis Obispo Airport (John Dagle), recently became an authorized dealer for the installation of the Jensen fittings and did a good job for me. One strut was rejected because of weakness due to internal rust, which is another well-known failure mode for our wing struts. With these strong forks I feel much more secure in turbulence and when otherwise pulling G-loads. The AD requiring Magnafluxing of the forks no longer applies. Also, the AD for inspecting the strut for internal damage was freshly complied with during the rework. Internal corrosion protection with Linoil was done. Reinspection in five years will be easy because it may be done visually through the large barrel sections installed for the larger diameter forks.

Fuel Management Dipstick

This is great. I can tell within about one half gallon how much fuel is remaining in a tank by using a calibrated clear plastic tube. I've eliminated many gas stops because of this reliable information. The dipstick I have is the "Universal Fuel Gauge" (Catalog #5304A)

Bill Kleinbauer's restored Pacer, based at the Hawthorne (California) Municipal Airport, is modified to allow the 1,950-pound gross weight, as per Piper Memo #35. This is the 125-hp version. (courtesy Bill Kleinbauer)

Full IFR panel of Bill Kleinbauer's PA-20 Pacer. (courtesy Bill Kleinbauer)

from Sporty's Pilot Shop. The tube is ½-inch outside diameter, and ¼-inch inside diameter, with a short plug in the bottom which has a ⅛-inch diameter hole in it. I have scratched gallon marks on the tube rather than use the calibration card that comes with it. That way, I can read the amount directly. These values are "total gallons," so make sure you subtract the approximately 1½ gallons unusable.

I have run tanks dry in level flight and it seems that unusable fuel is less than 1½ out of the 36 gallons total.

I have not worked too hard to use the levels in the fuel-level sight gauges below the tanks. The levels, of course, are different on the ground when the airplane is resting on the tailwheel, compared to the levels in flight at a level attitude. The white level marks seem to be in 2½-gallon increments, with five gallons remaining in the tank when the float tube bottoms out.

I have a tachometer with an hour meter that measures cumulative engine revolutions (an hour is defined as 2350 rpm). It turns out that, for cross-country flight, I consistently average 7.3 gallons of fuel consumption per tach hour. With 34.5 gallons of usable fuel, this gives 4.5+ tach hours of fuel on board.

Venturi-Driven Gyros

There was no engine-driven vacuum pump on the 125-hp O-290-D Lycoming in Two Six Kilo. I mounted the large-size venturi on the right side, aft of the engine cowling, and am using it very successfully to drive Sigma-Tech (formerly Edo-Air) attitude and directional gyros. No vacuum regulator was installed. Over five inches of suction is achieved at 123-mph cruising flight, so I may add a regulator to decrease pressure to five inches and eliminate over-revving. The gyros are functioning okay, due to vacuum from propwash before lift off from the runway. For backup, the turn needle instrument is electrically driven. The Pacer is so easy to fly on partial panel that I'm not overly concerned about venturi icing or AI and DG instrument malfunctions.

I might add one of the backup suction systems that can be connected with a shuttle valve to the engine intake manifold. At the moment, this is a low priority item. There is very little drift to the directional gyro. My gyros are not shock-mounted.

Maximum Allowable Gross Weight Increase

A good document to obtain to learn more about our Pipers is "Service Aids, Bulletins, Letters and Memos for Piper J-3 Through PA-22" from Univair, Aurora, Colorado. Service Memo #35 is titled "Piper Model PA-20 and PA-22 Increase in Gross Weight 1,800 to 1,950 lbs; Lycoming O-290-D Engine, 125 hp Only." This calls for a larger oil cooling radiator, different air scoop, and for the PA-20, a stronger tail spring clamp. I now have the equivalent of these mods. I called Piper Service in Lakeland, Florida, (Jim Crist) and was sent the revised Airplane Flight Manual, dated May 1952. The CG range changes are as follows:

FWD Limit Point No. 3: 17.5″ at 1,950 pounds (was 1,800 pounds)
RWD Limit: 24.0″ at 1,950 pounds (was 1,800 pounds)

So, more aft moment is permitted. I was not sent a new performance table and thus don't know how much the climb rate is degraded at the heavier weight. I gave Two Six Kilo a test recently. We flew three heavy passengers out to the Mojave (California) Airport to see the *Voyager* around-the-world non-refueled project (and to donate $150). We took publicity photos for my company newspaper at the Aerospace Corporation. The takeoff to return to L.A. was at 1:00 P.M., the temperature was near 100° F, and the airport altitude was about 3,000 feet MSL. I used 87 mph IAS, the handbook value for normal rate of climb with flaps up.

I was at 1,900 pounds and indicated a dismal 300-fpm climb rate. For 1,800 pounds gross the handbook shows 575 fpm at 3,000 feet and 100° F. I did manage to struggle up to 7,500 feet. I should have experimented with slower speeds and 10 degrees of flaps. Maybe next time; I did not want to overheat the engine.

Window Covers

Window covers keep the heat out and prevent curious eyes from viewing your radio panel. I made reflective covers for all windows and the windshield by cutting up a thin thermal cover that you can buy in sporting goods stores. Make paper patterns and lay them out on the cover before cutting. Velcro pieces can be used to mount the covers on the inside of the windows.

Hamilton Vertical Card Compass

I replaced the standard liquid float compass with the Hamilton Vertical Card Compass (from San-Val Discount Aircraft Parts, Van Nuys [California] Airport). I really like it; it looks and acts like a directional gyro and has better dampening than the float compass. Like the float compass, it does have lead/lag/acceleration errors and is not useful during steep-banked turns. It makes partial-panel IFR much easier for standard-rate turns and for holding headings. Passengers can handle the aircraft easier, too. I mounted it in place of the old compass on the flat surface above the center of the instrument panel.

Do develop calibration curves for it. I found that you don't need to raise the tail to level flight attitude to do this. Follow the instructions that come with the compass to set up the N-S-E-W trimming screws, while operating under the conditions given below.

1. 1800 rpm, all avionics on. This is the most common flight condition. Adjust screws for best compass accuracy.
2. 1800 rpm, avionics and electrical off. (I found this and #5 to give the same reading.)
3. 1800 rpm, all avionics on, and navigation lights on.
4. 1800 rpm, all avionics on, nav lights on, strobes or flashing beacon on.
5. No power, engine off, all avionics and electrical off. Tap the compass to ensure freedom of movement.

Plot the data to determine the five curve shapes and to check for errors. On the horizontal axis, show compass rose direction. On the vertical axis, show the compass correction amount required to get that direction. Put this information in tabular form and mount near your compass.

You can also do an airborne check of your compass accuracy using your directional gyro. Turn on all avionics, point in a known direction such as magnetic north, note if your compass is reading correctly, and set your gyro compass heading to your magnetic compass heading.

Turn to 90° on your gyro compass, achieve level flight, and read and record your magnetic compass value. Do the same at 180° and 270°, then back to magnetic north. These calibration tasks take time, but you'll be rewarded with a good knowledge of your key navigation aid.

Maintenance

In May of '84 I moved the plane to the Hawthorne Airport, which is only four miles from my house. At Hawthorne I put my name on the waiting list for a tiedown space with the city. The city charges $56 per month. For $65 per month I've been renting a nice spot behind their big hangar.

Fairly often, I fly to the Vandenberg AFB area on business. I land and stay in Lompoc, just seven miles from Vandenberg, and I've given my major aircraft maintenance chores to Lompoc Aviation (805-736-1273). Tom Brink is the A&P. He is great to deal with; friendly, smart, skilled, quality-oriented, honest ... and he tries to meet promised schedules. He has a side business of supplying aircraft-quality hardware (Genuine A/C Hardware, 805-736-2005). He did my last annual, took from January to April, and included overhaul of starter and generator, replacement of muffler, replacing sections of two rusted fuselage tubes, re-covering the belly and side fabric where these pieces were replaced, re-covering the right flap, replacing all control cables (probably the first time since new, 35 years ago), tail section disassembly to replace rusted forward pivot tube in the horizontal stabilizer, replacing tail brace wires and attachment hardware. He coordinated with John Dagle for retrofit of the Jensen strut forks, rerigging the wings, and overhaul of the carburetor air box mechanism.

Tom Brink and his assistant, Kevin Septer, do trust their own work. They flew with me to check the rigging and handling of the airplane after all that maintenance.

Windshield Replacement

I had my crazed windshield replaced by Lee Conlan of Homebuilt Aircraft (213-869-0536). He lives in Downey, but will pick up the new windshield from the manufacturer, Aircraft Windshield Company in Los Alamitos (213-430-8108), and will come to your aircraft if it is in or near the Los Angeles Basin. I prefer having this job done by a professional, since proper cutting and fitting are not easy. You don't want the windshield to crack while installing it, or afterwards due to poor technique. I replaced all of the side windows myself. The old windows were used as patterns, and the new ones were cut by a plexiglass supply store in Torrance (Gem-O-Lite Plastics, 213-539-8950). Perhaps a better way to ensure that you meet FAA standards would be to go to the Aircraft Windshield Company. They produce replacement windows and windshields for the J-3 through the PA-36, and have master patterns in house.

Weight and Balance

After all of the avionics and instrument changes, I decided to start with a fresh weight-and-balance sheet. A good place to do this in California is at Acme Aircraft at Torrance Airport where Roger Keeney presides (213-326-4081). He'll also go to your airport with his weighing equipment.

Two Six Kilo's original factory empty weight was 967 pounds. Now, as equipped, it weighs 1,006 pounds. So, with full fuel of 36 gallons (216 pounds), and full oil of seven quarts (15 pounds), I can carry 563 pounds of people and baggage for the original max gross of 1,800 pounds, or 713 pounds for the amended max gross of 1,950 pounds. Not bad.

Propeller Overhaul

The original prop, Sensenich M 76 AM-2, is still on Two Six Kilo and has 3,140 hours on it. To start off again on a good basis with such an important component, I had it overhauled at Torrance Airport by Aero Propeller (213-326-0560; ask for Ted). I understand that our props may be overhauled about four or five times. Some material is removed each time to resmooth the leading edges.

Maintenance Costs

Here are the 1985 prices and labor hours on some of my repair items. Shop labor is based on $35 per hour.

1.	Annual inspection	$280.00
2.	New muffler	332.00
3.	New muffler shroud	177.00(!)
4.	New voltage regulator	42.00
5.	Generator and starter overhaul	303.00
6.	Cylinder replacement	680.00
	(used cylinder, $200; overhaul, $281; rings, $79; pistons, $78; gaskets, $9; seal kit, $12; air freight for overhauled cylinder, $14)	
7.	Labor (12.5 hours)	375.00
8.	New rigging of wing and struts	5 hours
9.	New tail brace wires; replace stab inner sleeve	4 hours
10.	Replace rudder cables	.9 hour
11.	Replace elevator cables	1.7 hours
12.	Replace flap cables	1.5 hours
13.	Replace aileron cables	8.0 hours

14.	Replace corroded tubing under aft cabin floor	6.0 hours
15.	Replace corroded tubing left/forward door post	8.0 hours
16.	Replace fabric and finish items 14 and 15	16.0 hours
17.	Replace crankshaft forward seal (prop off)	.4 hour
18.	Re-cover one flap	8.0 hours

Fun Vacation Flights

In January '84, I flew up to San Francisco to participate in a workshop. I had a passenger, Ignacio Fernandez, born in Cuba, and an architect. He had never flown in a little airplane, and said that he always took a stiff drink before flying commercial. He really enjoyed our trip. I put him to work flying most of it.

My biggest problem on the flight was how to communicate using a 90-channel radio to get clearance to land at San Francisco International Airport. It was practically impossible. I ended up landing at San Carlos Airport, near the landing approach to SFO, then got tower-to-tower landing and takeoff instructions on a channel I could use. I made a high-speed landing and skidding turnoff to expedite my arrival. When we flew back to L.A. after the workshop, we remained at very low altitude along the spectacular California coastline, circled the migrating whales, and had lunch at Pismo Beach.

In May '84, I took three passengers on a week's vacation down the thousand-mile Baja Peninsula, all the way to the tip of Cabo San Lucas. On board with me were my girlfriend, Juliette Cuevas; my beautiful friend, Rianah Powers; and fellow engineer Roy Schermerhorn, who bravely answered my ad for passengers in the company paper.

The heaviest of us only weighed 140 pounds, so with full fuel tanks and 12 pounds of baggage each, we did not exceed the 1,800-pound max gross weight that was my standard then. This was a great flying vacation . . . the Baja fly-in resorts are my favorite spots in the world, and I highly recommend such a getaway. I've been down there six times in the past 25 years. Use Arnold Senterfitt's book, *Airports of Mexico and Central America* to guide you.

In September '84, I flew a coworker, Dave Walters, over to his resort in Lakeside, near Show Low, Arizona, which is up in the White Mountains area, northeast of Phoenix. On the return from Show Low, I reinforced in my mind the value of carrying a "Little John" for bladder relief in flight. I did not have one, did have too much coffee for breakfast, and had to make an emergency diving descent from 8,500 feet to land for a quick pit stop at Buckeye, Arizona. This added one extra stop to the return flight.

The Little John, available from Sporty's Pilot Shop, is good to carry with your flight equipment. Take it to the airport filled with clean water for rinsing the dust off your airplane's windshield during your preflight tasks.

Speaking of windshield care, I use water and my hand to flush off the dust and grit with gentle, vertical strokes, making sure that I don't scratch circular swirl marks into the plexiglass—marks that are so bad for visibility when flying or landing into the sunset. Use an old, clean, cotton-based T-shirt or towel to dry the glass after the rinse. This prevents spotting. Once in a while, I use a cleaner inside and out on the windshield and windows. The cleaner I like best is Brillianize. Compared to Mirror Glaze, it's easier and cheaper, and doesn't leave a greasy residue to wipe off.

I did go to the May 11, 1985 second fly-in of the newly formed Southwestern Pacific Chapter of the Short Wing Piper Club. It was held at Lake Isabella, in the mountains northeast of Bakersfield. Lee Berry and his wife, Pat, flew down from the San Francisco area and planned to stay overnight in a motel in nearby Kernville. I was not ready to hit-and-run, either. Most attendees came, ate, talked, and flew away. Some camped at the airport in the wind and dust. The Berrys and I got rooms at a motel on a hillside overlooking the Kern River and its rafting adventurers.

We ate dinner and breakfast together. I suggested that, since they were on vacation for a few days, they visit Catalina Island. We flew in formation to there, and landed on the "Airport in the Sky" under the low clouds. The airport is like a carrier deck at 1,600 feet MSL.

We were going to share a lunch of buffaloburgers at the airport, but the minibus was ready to leave for the town of Avalon, so we said quick goodbyes instead. They stayed at a resort and liked the island so well that they remained an extra day. Lee is certainly a big booster for the Pipers and the Short Wing Piper Club.

Piper Clipper, (PA-16)
Specifications and Performance

Engine	Lyc O-235-C1
Hp and rpm.	115 @ 2800
Gross weight (lbs.).	1650
Empty weight (lbs.).	850
Wingspan (ft.).	29.25
Wing area (sq./ft.).	147.5
Length (ft.).	20.1
Height (in.).	74
Propeller diameter (in.).	73
Power loading (lbs./hp).	16.2
Wing loading (lbs. sq./ft.).	11.2
Baggage capacity (lbs.).	50
Tire pressure (lbs. sq./in.).	22
Maximum speed (mph).	125
Cruising speed (mph).	112
Stalling speed (mph).	50
Rate of climb (initial; ft./min.).	600
Service ceiling (ft.).	11,000
Absolute ceiling (ft.).	13,500
Cruising range (statute mi.).	480
Takeoff run (ft.).	720
Fuel consumption (gal./hr.).	7

Piper Pacer (PA-20)
Specifications and Performance

	PA-20-125	PA-20-135
Engine	Lyc O-290-D	Lyc O-290-D2
Hp and rpm.	125 @ 2600	135 @ 2600
Gross weight (lbs.).	1800	1950
Empty weight (lbs.).	970	1020
Useful load (lbs.).	830	930
Wingspan (ft.).	29.3	29.3
Wing area (sq. ft.).	147.5	147.5
Length (ft.).	20.4	20.4
Height (in.).	74.5	74.5
Propeller diameter (max. in.).	74	74
Power loading (lbs./hp).	14.4	14.4
Wing loading (lbs./sq. ft.).	12.2	13.2
Baggage capacity (lbs.).	50	50
Fuel capacity (U.S. gal.).	36	36
Tire pressure (lbs. sq./in.).	20	20
Maximum speed (mph).	135	139
Cruise (mph; 75% power @ SL).	125	125
Cruise (mph; 75% power @ 7000 ft.).		134
Stalling speed (mph).	48	48*
Takeoff run (ft.).	1372	1220*
Landing roll (ft.).	500	500*
Rate of climb (initial; ft./min.).	810	620
Service ceiling (ft.).	14,250	15,000
Cruising range (statute mi.).	580	580

*Flaps extended.

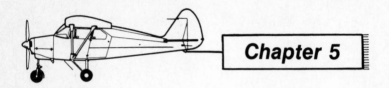

Chapter 5

The Tri-Pacer
and Colt

The Piper PA-22 Tri-Pacer was introduced in 1952 and remained
in production through 1960. Early Tri-Pacers were powered with
the 125-hp O-290-D Lycoming engine, then the 135-hp O-290-D2.
By 1959, the Caribbean model had the 150-hp O-320 engine, while
the Standard and Super Custom Tri-Pacers were fitted with the
Lycoming O-320-B rated at 160 hp. Prices ranged from $8,395 to
$10,770, depending upon engine installation and the usual extra-cost
options. A total of 7,668 Tri-Pacers were built.

THE PA-22 TRI-PACER

The Tri-Pacers are docile and easy to fly in the tradition of their
generation of Pipers. Checking an old notebook in which I recorded
a flight in Niner Seven Three Niner Delta, a 1959 Caribbean (in order to write about it at the time), I find some useful numbers. This
account was for a new student pilot on his/her first lesson, and I'll
pick it up near the end of the pre-flight inspection:

> . . . Reaching beneath the nose, at the rear of the engine, open
> the little petcock which drains the fuel sediment bowl. Then, just
> inboard of the right landing gear strut on the plane's belly, there's
> a small opening with another petcock. It drains the fuel line at its lowest

Three-Niner-Delta is a 1959 Caribbean model of the Tri-Pacer series, fitted with the 150-hp O-320 Lycoming, and priced (new) at $8,395.

point, so empty that ounce or so of gasoline on the ground also . . .

You'll sit in the pilot's seat on the left. Put your foot on the step and, with your right hand, grasp the brace behind the windshield and swing into the seat. Do not pull yourself in by the control wheel. Now fasten your seat belt. Comfortable? Okay. Here is the pre-start procedure:

Be sure the parking brake is set. The brake lever is below the instrument panel, just under the throttle. To set the brakes, pull the lever back and then pull out the "brake set" knob on the lower instrument panel just to the left of the control wheel.

The master switch is a toggle-type and is below your left leg on the front of the seat. Snap it up to turn it on. This will cause your fuel gauges to register.

The fuel tank selector switch is on the left kick-pad below the instrument panel. Its positions are LEFT, RIGHT, and OFF. Turn it to the tank which you are to use—the fullest one.

Push the fuel mixture knob completely in. This gives you a rich mixture, which is desirable on takeoffs and landings. This knob is at the bottom of the instrument panel on your right.

Set your altimeter and instrument panel clock.

Above the windshield is a crank with an indicator reading "Nose—Up, Down." This is the stabilizer control. Set it in neutral.

The carburetor heat control is directly in front of you on the instrument panel. Set it at "cold" . . .

Master switch still on? Okay, just beneath it is the starter button [use of the primer is also explained at this point].

Open your window and call, "Clear!"

With the throttle knob in the palm of your right hand, place your forefinger along the throttle shaft with your nail about an eighth of an inch from the friction lock. Now, push in the throttle just that much. Almost no throttle is needed to start the engine. Press the starter button with your left hand and simultaneously reach to the instrument panel with your right hand, turning the magnet switch to "BOTH."

A proper idle is explained, the importance of the oil pressure and temperature gauges mentioned, and then moving along the taxi strip, the student is advised to keep the right hand on the throttle and the left hand in his/her lap in the beginning as a reminder that the nosewheel is linked to the rudder pedals.

On the run-up pad just short of the runway, the usual pre-takeoff checks are made—mags checked at 1,700 rpm with a 100-rpm drop allowable on each—and because visibility from the Tri-Pacer is so poor, I advise that the airplane be turned in a complete circle on the run-up pad to check the traffic pattern for incoming aircraft (we're assuming no tower).

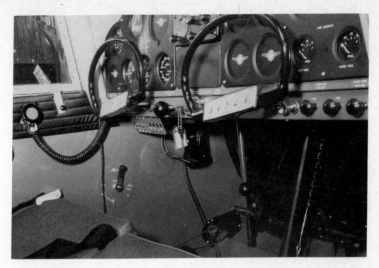

Tri-Pacer interior. The "Johnson Bar" protruding from beneath the instrument panel activates main brakes simultaneously (no brakes on the rudder pedals). The fuel selector is on the left kick-pad, while the master switch and starter button are behind the pilot's leg on front of the left seat.

Tracking down the runway centerline at full throttle, we ease into the air as soon as there is good response to the elevators. No given speed is mentioned because the student's eyes should be outside the cabin, not trying to find the airspeed indicator on the

The altimeter, tachometer, and vertical-speed indicator are across the bottom of the panel; airspeed and turn/bank are at upper left. This machine was produced before the T-grouping of flight instruments was conceived—and before the spring-loaded starter switch was added to the magneto switches.

still-unfamiliar panel. Actually, the Tri-Pacer likes to fly at about 60 mph (indicated) on an average day with two aboard. She will get off sooner, but there's no point in it.

After the student is reminded to use more rudder to compensate for torque/P-factor at this throttle setting, it is suggested that airspeed be adjusted with the control wheel for a 90-mph climbout. Usually, that results in about 800 fpm for the first couple of thousand feet, and erodes quite slowly after that. We don't often go to 7,000 feet, where this machine is most efficient. This is the year 1960, and we don't unnecessarily complicate things.

The Tri-Pacer stalls reluctantly. Power off (I should say, with engine idling, zero thrust) and stick all the way back, she will mush downward at 800 fpm or more. Adequate aileron remains. Although the break is almost imperceptible, you can feel the airplane shudder as the air burbles over the wing. You will, of course, get a more definite break in power-on stalls.

I've been told—although I have never tried it—that both the Tri-Pacer and the Colt will roll inverted and enter a spin from a power-on stall in a turn with 30 degrees or more of bank. Personally, I think you would have to have the controls crossed with a lot of back pressure on the yoke to get such a result. Even the best-mannered airplane will rebel if sufficiently abused.

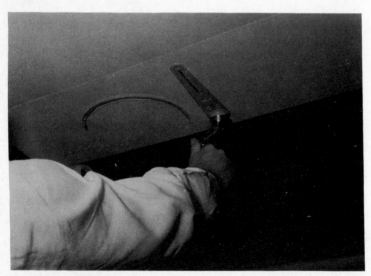

The Tri-Pacer's stabilizer trim is literally cranked in, a common installation on early cabin airplanes.

Jeff Clausen of Lincoln, Nebraska, with a Tri-Pacer that sports an original paint scheme and no clue as to model or engine installation. Altogether, 7,668 Tri-Pacers were built from 1952 through 1960. (courtesy Jeff Clausen)

Power-off glides are best accomplished with the engine at a fast idle, adjusting airspeed with the yoke at about 80 mph indicated, then trimming away the control pressure with four or five turns of the stabilizer crank toward the ''Nose Up'' arrow. The secret of gliding a Tri-Pacer is to keep the speed up, which becomes obvious if you get too slow (the sink rate quickly becomes unacceptable). This is a good trait when it is desirable to get rid of excess altitude within a relatively short distance.

Landings in the Tri-Pacer are equally straightforward. The flaps help a little, and these airplanes do nice forward slips without flaps. Seventy-five miles per hour is a good approach speed using flaps, with the flare at about 10 feet and touchdown on the mains at about 60 mph. Unless you have a pronounced crosswind to deal with, hold the nosewheel off as long as practicable. Aerodynamic braking from a high angle of attack (with the mains rolling) is cheaper than tromping the binders. The Tri-Pacer's brakes aren't all that good, anyway.

The Tri-Pacer runs out of rudder too soon as the speed bleeds off, which may be the reason that Piper limited the up elevator travel so much. At least one fellow I know who is making a Pacer of his Tri-Pacer is modifying the upper elevator stop to get more up elevator travel, but I don't know whether or not there is an STC for that.

Dale Andrews, a Littleton, Colorado, oil company land manager, and his 1959 Tri-Pacer. Dale's machine has 160 hp, full IFR panel, and has been re-covered with Stits Poly-Fiber, finished in red-and-white with gold trim. (courtesy Dale P. Andrews)

Owning a Tri-Pacer

Dale P. Andrews is a Littleton, Colorado, businessman who owns a Tri-Pacer and does a little aviation writing when he has the time. The following are excerpts from one of Dale's articles in the *Short Wing Piper News*.

In early October, I went out to Denver Centennial Airport to pick up a rented Cessna 182 for a business trip. With my Tri-Pacer, *Topher II*, strung all over Lonnie McLaughlin's hangar for an annual, and with the engine being 80 miles north in Fort Collins, I had to face the fact that I'd be renting an airplane for the next month or two.

Actually, with this trip it was not all bad because the increased airspeed and performance of the 182 would come in handy for the long day I had planned.

When I arrived at the airport, I found an airplane loaded with snow and ice, due to a storm that had come through Denver a couple of days before. Yesterday's sun had been sufficient to melt only part of the snow and leave a solid cake of ice on the airplane. It wasn't a big load of ice, and since I had lots of horsepower and was flying solo, I was tempted to just take off and let the ice knock itself off in the flight north to Riverton, Wyoming. Fortunately, however, I found myself falling back on long-ingrained habits. If you are going to be in this flying game and want to be in it for a long time, you do things right—and "right" meant spending $42 to have the airplane de-iced so I could make a timely departure and meet my appointment.

Leaving Denver at 8:30 in the morning, I flew north out of Colorado into Wyoming, and then northwest across Laramie and Pathfinder Reservoir to Riverton, where I met with officials of the Bureau of Indian Affairs concerning some oil and gas leases. After lunch and additional meetings with people from the BIA, I hopped back into the airplane and headed home to Denver, arriving at 4:00 P.M., in time to get home before the evening traffic buildup.

By checking the commuter airlines that service Riverton, I found that such a trip would have taken me two to three hours longer, door-to-door, and would have cost approximately the same as the rental charge on the 182. I think this is encouraging—it can still be economical to use a lightplane for business. Mind you, you have to be wise as you select your use of a light airplane. Unless you intend to make a long trip as part business and part recreation, it may be wiser to take commercial airlines.

In doing some calculating, taking the same trip to Riverton in my Tri-Pacer would have required probably an hour and a half longer round-trip, because the 182 is significantly faster. However, even in my Tri-Pacer I would have at least met, if not beaten, the door-to-door time via commuter airline, and somewhere in all this we have to count the fun factor. In fact, I also have to admit to myself that pleasure is the reason I would have flown the Tri-Pacer rather than the 182 because there is something about the pride of ownership that goes with this business of owning a short-wing Piper.

I think it is important to be honest with ourselves about that which we can and cannot practically do with our airplanes, and it is important to admit that pleasure plays a significant part in owning and flying our airplanes. We need not be ashamed that this is true, because relaxation is sought by all of us in many different ways, and those of us who choose to call sitting in a rag-wing airplane flying across country relaxing—and perhaps also have the advantage of using it as a business tool—are indeed most fortunate.

Decisions at Annual

As I was sitting in the 182 with the autopilot doing the flying, I mentally congratulated myself for having the ice removed from the airplane before flying it, and then my thoughts floated back to a decision I had made in September, when it was time for my Tri-Pacer to go in for its annual inspection. Having recently purchased the airplane, I realized that I didn't know a whole lot about it, other than what the logbooks showed, and the pre-purchase inspection by a mechanic. When you own an airplane such as a short-wing Piper, with bluebook values low compared to other airplanes, the price of an annual is not lightly regarded. The $500 to $1,000 cost of an annual on this airplane is high when compared to the same cost for an annual on a $30,000 machine. For that reason, there is a temptation to try to cut corners when it comes to such things as annual inspections and even routine maintenance. I think this is most dangerous, and as I dwelt on how I was going to approach my annual, I thought of ways I could keep my costs down, but had to admit that some of the things I was considering were frankly both dangerous and illegal.

There are ways that you may cut costs of an annual inspection without doing anything dangerous or illegal. One is finding a competent mechanic who will allow you to participate in order to cut his time and therefore the dollars spent. [Author's note: A highly competent but grumpy mechanic once told me that the price of an annual would be $50 extra if I wanted to help.]

The major decision I made at that time was that I would turn my airplane over to one of several mechanics I know who are experts on the short-wing Pipers. For many, such a decision may mean taking their airplanes some distance, because we are dealing with what is becoming a rare breed . . . I was fortunate that in the Denver area there are two or three very capable mechanics who are short-wing Piper owners and who have a love for the birds.

The mechanic I chose, mostly because he is located on my airfield, was Mr. Lonnie McLaughlin of the Associates Flying Club. Lonnie owns a Tri-Pacer, is a member of the Short Wing Piper Club, and, next to his wife and family, probably loves his Tri-Pacer, *Songbird,* more than anything else.

As we talked about him doing the annual on *Topher II,* he emphasized to me that the only way he would do it would be to do it right. To ask him to cut corners was to ask him to compromise his license and his integrity. That was not fair to him, me, or my family. With that in mind, I turned him loose, and believe you me, you would be amazed at what he found needed to be done in an airplane that had been reasonably well maintained, with what I thought were adequate logbook entries and documents.

A couple of times, Lonnie would call and say that he had found this or that which needed to be taken care of, and deep down inside me would well up the desire to say, "Can't we overlook it until the next annual?" But then I came back to how I would feel if someone asked me to professionally compromise myself in my business so they could save a few dollars. Then I thought about Pattie and the kids; they would be riding in the airplane with me. And all of a sudden I decided that the airplane might have to sit on the ground an extra month or so until I could get the money together, but the job would be done right.

I am writing this not without some pain because the financial sacrifices I have made have been considerable, and quite literally the airplane is sitting in the hangar right now, not yet completed, while

I wait to get the money together, but I know one thing: When the time comes to put the cowl back on *Topher II* and take it into the blue Colorado sky, I will do so with confidence.

Firewall Forward

One of the things we discovered during the annual was that there were some metal shavings in the oil on the suction screen which were not there during the pre-purchase inspection. The decision as to what to do with the engine was an easy one for me because of a previous experience I had with Firewall Forward, a repair shop in Fort Collins, Colorado. Having had them overhaul an engine for me at one time, I knew of their outstanding service and unusual integrity. Therefore, my engine was shipped to Mark at Firewall Forward for inspection. Here again, knowing a competent mechanic made my decision easier.

I did not give Mark carte blanche to go through the engine and completely spend my next year's salary rebuilding it. I asked him to determine what it would take, within reason, to fix the engine so that it would be safe and give maximum performance. You realize, when you do something like this you are placing yourself in the hands of your mechanic, not unlike the way you do when you place yourself in the hands of your doctor. In this case, this trust is paying off, as Mark is repairing the engine at a reasonable cost, without compromising quality or safety.

I guess my point is that when flying airplanes that have been out of production for some time, it is important that we cultivate our relationships and do some investigating when it comes to deciding who we'll allow to maintain our machines and keep them airworthy.

Winter Flying in the Rockies

We are now well into fall with winter approaching. In the Denver area we have had two or three snowstorms to remind us that the white stuff is not far away. Those of us who own and fly short-wing Pipers in the Rocky Mountain region generally look upon the fall and winter seasons with positive feelings. When you are flying out of airports with 5,000 feet and higher elevations, density altitudes get very high very quickly on hot summer days. As the air cools with fall and winter, we find new life springing into our airplane as the propeller gets a better bite on the air and the wing works more efficiently. It's fun to find the airplane coming off the runway sooner than it did for the last few months, and it's fun to see the rate-of-climb indicator move from 300 or 400 fpm to 500 or 600 fpm. In many ways, I consider winter flying in my Tri-Pacer safer than summer flying simply because of the increased performance I receive in the colder air.

With both summer and winter flying, there are adjustments that need to be made when flying this country. In the summer, you take precautions with density altitude and rate of climb, and you watch

The Piper brochure promoting the 1959 Caribbean claimed a 132-mph cruise. I always figured 125 mph for cross-country (between 1,000 and 5,000 feet) and encountered no surprises. Some owners today are converting to Pacer configuration, but it is not true that all you have to do is turn the mains around to accomplish this.

Andrews' Tri-Pacer has 1300 hours TT since new. Avionics include dual nav-coms, glide slope, transponder, and audio panel with marker beacon. (courtesy Dale P. Andrews)

closer for updrafts and downdrafts as you fly the ridges of the mountains. In winter, you tend to concentrate more on taking care of your engine during startup, making sure snow and ice are off the airplane before you depart, and determining that the survival gear you carry is adequate to keep you warm should you have to go down somewhere. Those of us who are not fortunate enough to have hangarage for our aircraft will have to be especially careful to keep our eyes on freely moving control surfaces, wheels inside wheel pants, and other components that could get jammed with water that melts, runs down, and then freezes.

There is something exhilarating about letting the little bird lift off, heading in the direction of the snow-capped peaks, and feeling the solid lift in the wings. For us Rocky Mountain pilots, winter is when we get the chance to feel our airplanes perform as those of you who live at sea level experience it all the time. Therefore, I think we fly more in winter than do our fellow pilots in the flatlands. Those who are fortunate enough to hangar their machines in this area may find the hardest part of winter flying to be the drive to the airport on icy roads; once airborne, it is a lot of fun, and absolutely beautiful.

Tri-Pacers, Generally Speaking

In the mid-1970s, a good Tri-Pacer could be found in the used market for as little as $4,000, but by 1986 the prices ranged from twice that up to $12,000. In fact, there was a super slick Tri-Pacer, loaded with goodies, offered for $14,000 in an issue of the *Short Wing Piper News*.

I regard the Tri-Pacer as easy to fly, with absolutely no surprises, except that with power off it doesn't have much of a glide at low airspeeds. Get the nose down and maintain the IAS at 80 and it glides pretty well. So, it ain't exactly a sailplane, but if you take note of the wings' aspect ratio, you'll find the craft to be a "short-wing" Piper.

Back in 1959, I worked with veteran flight instructor Clay Johnson to produce a basic little book on flying called *Your Pilot's License*. In the first edition, we used a new 150-hp Tri-Pacer Caribbean model, Three Niner Delta, for all of the illustrations in the book, and I spent many happy hours in that machine. I hope she's got a good home.

For student instruction, 2,000 rpm would consume about seven gallons of fuel per hour (80/87 octane), and the airplane was approved for spins when operated in the utility category with a maximum gross of 1,680 pounds.

THE PA-22-108 COLT

The Piper Colt utilizes the Tri-Pacer airframe fitted with the 108-hp Lycoming O-235 engine. In place of the Tri-Pacer's rear seat is one very large baggage bin which is limited to 100 pounds of baggage. However, this neat little two-placer has a useful load of 710 pounds, which means that it will carry two large people more than 600 miles nonstop at a bit over 100 mph in the lower altitudes.

As you would expect, this airplane flies very much like a Tri-Pacer; there is only a 160-pound difference in empty weights. The smaller engine is most noticeable during takeoff and climb, while cruise is about 20 mph slower in the 3,000-to-5,000-foot range, where most owners seem to fly these machines.

This aircraft is ready to fly at 60 mph on takeoff; initial climb will be between 600 and 700 fpm at 75 to 80 mph. Approaches are made at the same speed (the Colt does not have flaps), with touchdown at about 65 mph. As with the Tri-Pacer, you need to mind your rudder in turns.

There seems to be a widespread belief that you can make a tailwheel airplane out of a Colt by simply mounting the main gear backwards and removing the nosewheel. Be advised, my fellow aeronauts, it won't fit. You can convert the Colt to a tailwheel airplane, but be sure and get the STC for it from the Short Wing Piper Club, and do it right.

The most important Airworthiness Directive, which applies to

The Piper PA-22-108 Colt might be the most sport airplane for the money in today's used market. With 108 hp, the two-place Colt will transport 700 pounds of people, fuel, and baggage nearly 700 miles at slightly over 100 mph.

all PA-22s, is one that requires checking the wing struts for rust.

The Colt was offered in three versions, Standard, Custom, and Super Custom, priced from $4,995 to $6,995, with additional instruments, radio, wheel pants, aux fuel, etc., determining the model. A total of 1,822 were produced.

Construction of the PA-22s was the same as the earlier fabric-covered Pipers—welded chrome moly steel tubing for the fuselage frame, dural spars and stamped metal ribs in the wings. Covering was aircraft-grade cotton (long staple), which was required by the CAA/FAA to test not less than 80 psi both warp and fill (both directions) when new, and no less than 56 psi in service. The finish was cellulose acetate butyrate (CAB) dope over an initial coating of cellulose nitrate dope. According to Piper Service Memo #25, issued in 1954, these airplanes received a total of 11 coats of dope—six of clear for filler, two of silver for ultraviolet protection of the fabric, and three of color.

The Colt may be the best two-placer for the money in today's used market. Introduced in 1960 and produced into 1963, the Colt was fitted with the 108-hp Lycoming O-235 and priced at $4,995. Employing the basic Tri-Pacer airframe, the Colt has a useful load of around 700 pounds with rear seats and rear door removed depending upon equipment added. That means it will handle two full-sized adults, 100 pounds of baggage, and full fuel (36 gallons).

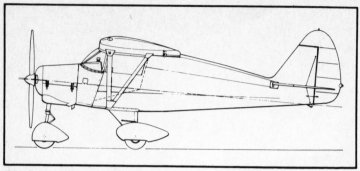

The Colt is easy to fly and inexpensive to maintain. A total of 1,822 were produced from 1960 through 1963.

Except for the lack of flaps, this machine is operated just like the Tri-Pacer. The master switch is in the same "secret" location under the pilot's seat, the starter is engaged by turning the key all the way to the right (just like your car), and the brakes (like those of the unmodified Tri-Pacers) are simultaneously activated by the "Johnson bar" that protrudes from beneath the center of the instrument panel. Also, like the Tri-Pacer, the Colt's binders are not the best you've ever used—which is why so many PA-22s you'll see nowadays have toe brakes.

In flight, this machine behaves like its four-place sister. Stalling speed is a little high in relation to cruise—somewhere just below 60 mph indicated (hard to tell because you've always got the airspeed needle bouncing around in a full stall). In any event, this airplane doesn't want to break cleanly when stalled power-off. It very definitely quits flying, however, and will mush downward with the nose fairly high and the wings level. Power-on and accelerated stalls do produce a definite break, although there isn't much aerodynamic warning.

The Tri-Pacers were equipped at the factory with a light spring load between aileron and rudder to help counteract the airplane's adverse yaw tendency in a turn, but many owners have removed this artificial coordinator. Apparently, the Colts were not rigged with this interconnection and require simultaneous stick and rudder for the initiation of turns. That's the way it should be. Positive control is the secret of safe flight, rather than coordination at all costs. You can fly the well-known Death Spiral all the way into eternity with aileron and rudder perfectly coordinated.

No one seems to slip an airplane anymore, flaps—and runways that stretch into the next county—make slips unnecessary. It seems that all you have to do is get reasonably close to the ground, shut your eyes, and wait for the airplane to land itself. That, of course, assumes a tricycle landing gear. You can't do it that way in an airplane with the nosewheel under the tail, especially in a short-coupled Piper ragwing. When landing a tailwheel airplane, you've got to pay attention.

Many Colts and Tri-Pacers are being transformed into tailwheel airplanes. In fact, these airplanes have suffered a number of approved modifications (Supplemental Type Certificates). For further information, contact:

> Mr. Larry D. Smith
> Membership Chairman
> The Short Wing Piper Club
> Route #11, 708 W. Annie Drive,
> Munice, IN 47302
> (317) 298-5487 evenings

The Short Wing Piper Club is a most effective clearing house for all matters pertaining to these great aircraft.

Piper Tri-Pacer
Specifications and Performance

	PA-22-125	PA-22-135
Engine	Lyc O-290-D	Lyc O-290-D2
Hp and rpm	125 @ 2600	135 @ 2600
Gross weight (lbs.)	1800	1950
Empty weight (lbs.)	1000	1060
Useful load (lbs.)	800	890
Wingspan (ft.)	29.3	29.3
Wing area (sq. ft.)	147.5	147.5
Length (ft.)	20.4	20.4
Height (in.)	100	100
Propeller diameter (max. in.)	74	74
Power loading (lbs./hp)	14.4	14.4
Wing loading (lbs./sq. ft.)	12.2	13.2
Baggage capacity (lbs.)	50	50
Fuel capacity (U.S. gal.)	36	36
Tire pressure (mains; lbs.)	20	22
Maximum speed (mph)	133	137
Cruise (75% power @ sea level)	123	123
Cruise (75% power @ 7000 ft.)	128	132
Stalling speed (flaps extended)	48	48*
Takeoff roll (ft.)	1372	1220*
Takeoff over 50 ft. obstacle	1788	1600*
Landing roll (ft.)	500	500*
Best rate of climb speed (mph)	84	84
Rate of climb (ft./min.)	810	620
Best angle of climb (mph)	- -	70
Best angle of climb (ratio)	- -	1:11
Service ceiling (ft.)	14,250	15,000
Absolute ceiling	16,250	17,500
Fuel consumption (gal./hr.)	7.7	7.7
Cruising range (statute mi.)	580	570

*Flaps Extended.

Piper Tri-Pacer Specifications and Performance

	PA-22-150	PA-22-160
Engine	Lyc O-320	Lyc O-320-B
Hp and rpm.	150 @ 2700	160 @ 2700
Gross weight (lbs.).	2000	2000
Empty weight (lbs.).	1100	1110
Useful load (lbs.).	900	890
Wingspan (ft.).	29.3	29.3
Wing area (sq. ft.).	147.5	147.5
Length (ft.).	20.6	20.6
Height (in.).	100	100
Propeller diameter (max. in.).	74	74
Power loading (lbs./hp).	13.3	12.5
Wing loading (lbs./sq. ft.).	13.5	13.5
Baggage capacity (lbs.).	100	100
Fuel capacity (std, U.S. gal.).	36	36
Fuel capacity (optional).	44	44
Tire pressure (lbs. mains/nose).	22/15	22/15
Maximum speed (mph).	139	141
Cruise (75% power @ sea level).	123	125
Cruise (75% power @ 7000 ft.).	132	134
Stalling speed (mph).	49*	49*
Takeoff roll (ft.).	1220*	1120*
Takeoff over 50-ft. obstacle.	1600*	1480*
Landing roll (ft.).	500*	500*
Best rate of climb speed (mph).	84	84
Rate of climb (ft./min.).	725	800
Best angle of climb speed (mph).	70	70
Best angle of climb (ratio).	1:11	1:10
Service ceiling (ft.).	15,000	16,500
Absolute ceiling (ft.).	17,500	19,000
Fuel consumption (gal./hr.).	9	9
Cruising range (standard tanks).	492	500
Cruising range (optional tanks).	600	610

*Flaps extended

Piper Tri-Pacer Floatplane
Specifications and Performance

	PA-22-150	PA-22-160
Engine	Lyc O-320	Lyc O-320-B
Hp and rpm	150 @ 2700	160 @ 2700
Gross weight (lbs.)	1950	1950
Empty weight (lbs.)	1280	1290
Useful load (lbs.)	670	660
Wingspan (ft.)	29.3	29.3
Wing area (sq. ft.)	147.5	147.5
Length (ft.)	22	22
Height (in.)	103	103
Propeller diameter (max. in.)	74	74
Power loading (lbs./hp)	13	12.2
Wing loading (lbs./sq. ft.)	13.2	13.2
Baggage capacity (lbs.)	100	100
Fuel capacity (standard, U.S. gal.)	36	36
Fuel capacity (optional)	44	44
Maximum speed (mph)	115	117
Cruise (75% power @ sea level)	105	107
Cruise (75% power @ 7000 ft.)	110	112
Stalling speed (mph)	58	58
Best rate of climb speed (mph)	75	75
Rate of climb (ft./min.)	675	750
Best angle of climb speed (mph)	65	65
Best angle of climb (ratio)	1:9	1:9
Service ceiling (ft.)	13,850	15,300
Absolute ceiling (ft.)	16,200	17,500
Fuel consumption (gal./hr.)	9	9
Cruising range (standard tanks)	420*	430*
Cruising range (optional tanks)	515*	525*

*Statute miles

Performance figures are for standard airplanes flown at gross weight under standard conditions at sea level.

Piper Colt PA-22-108
Specifications and Performance

Engine	Lyc O-235-C1
Hp and rpm.	108 @ 2600
Gross weight (lbs.).	1650
Empty weight (lbs.).	940
Useful load (lbs.).	710
Wingspan (ft.).	29.3
Wing area (sq./ft.).	147.5
Length (ft.).	20.2
Height (in.).	100
Power loading (lbs./hp).	15.28
Wing loading (lbs. sq./ft.).	11.19
Baggage capacity (lbs.).	100
Propeller diameter (in.).	76
Fuel capacity (U.S. gal.).	36
Maximum speed (mph).	120
Cruising speed (mph).	108
Stalling speed (mph).	56
Climb rate (initial; ft./min.).	610
Service ceiling (ft.).	12,000
Cruising range (statute mi.).	690

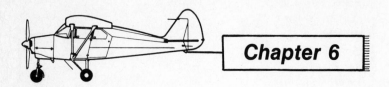

Chapter 6

Wag-Aero's
"Shadow Pipers"

Three years after learning to fly, Dick Wagner started an aircraft supply business with a single item he had invented himself. Dick was 20 years old, and the item was a simple rubber plug that sealed inspection holes for Luscombe wing spars. That was some 30 years ago, and in the meantime Wagner has progressed to the left seat of a Northwest Airlines DC-10 while he and wife Bobbie have built their aircraft supply business, Wag-Aero, Inc., into one of the nation's largest for amateur plane builders and classic aircraft restorers. In recent years Wagner has developed three homebuilts that are at once replicas and improved versions of the J-3, PA-14, and PA-17 Pipers.

THE SPORT TRAINERS

The Wagners have had a little trouble deciding what to call their airplanes—which are available as plans only, partial kits, or complete kits. The J-3 Cub lookalike came first, back in 1970, and was referred to as the "Reverse Cub," and then the "CUBy." They finally settled on "Sport Trainer." Next came the "Wag-A-Bond," a "shadow" of the Piper PA-15/17, which practically named itself. In 1982 the "CHUBy CUBy" (good grief!) was introduced, and has since been renamed "Sportsman 2+2" (you coulda done better on that one, folks).

The Wag-Aero Sport Trainer, available in five versions, is a replica of the Piper J-3 Cub. Finding a proper engine for this homebuilt can be the builder's biggest problem. (courtesy Wag-Aero)

The Sport Trainer is available in five versions:

- A replica of the Piper J-3, but with a 180-pound higher gross weight and 40 pounds more empty weight than the original J-3C-65. The Wag-Aero machine will accept engines up to and including the 100-hp Continental O-200.
- The Sport Trainer Model 11, intended as a replica of the Piper PA-11 Cub Special. This version has a full cowling for adapting Lycoming O-235 and O-290-D engines.
- The Acro Trainer, based on the Reed Clip-Wing Cub STC (which Wag-Aero owns), with shortened wings and beefed-up fuselage. It will accept engines through 150 hp (i.e., the O-320), and uses the standard Sport Trainer drawings, plus Acro Trainer wing supplement drawings.
- The Super Sport, a floatplane designed for a full cowl and 150 hp.
- The Observer, similar to the Piper L-21 with provision for a military-style greenhouse and any engine up to 150 hp. It's built from standard drawings with Observer supplements.

As mentioned above, you can purchase plans only and then scrounge for materials, including any original Cub components you can find, and which the FAA will allow you to use. The rule for homebuilts is supposed to be that they are at least 51 percent constructed by the amateur builder.

For a while, the FAA was pretty mean about allowing the use of component parts from commercially produced airplanes to make a homebuilt, because some people were assembling airplanes completely from wings, tails, fuselages, etc., taken from various wrecks. Nowadays, the FAA doesn't monitor the homebuilt aircraft scene as closely as it once did. This is partly because the amateur plane builders have proven to be quite responsible over the years, but there are negative reasons for this as well. In the mid-1980s, the FAA is understaffed and morale is poor. The FAA has, in fact, been going downhill ever since Lyndon Johnson stripped it of agency status and stuffed it into the Department of Transportation.

My point is, some FARs are stretched a little these days, and the extent to which you may use scrounged Piper parts to build a home-constructed airplane is going to be up to the individual FAA inspector at your General Aviation District Office (GADO).

You can buy a complete kit, all at once, for any of the Wag-Aero airplanes, or you can buy the sub-kits one at a time, which is probably the best way to go. It takes about 15 sub-kits to build a Sport Trainer. Also offered are labor-saving kits, such as wing kits with stamped aluminum ribs (you make your own wing ribs of wood using the regular kit), pre-welded fuselage, prefab tail, landing gear, etc. Again, just where any given FAA inspector draws the line on prefab components in the interest of preserving the 51 percent rule is hard to say. But you and the inspector should have a complete understanding on this before building, or you'll risk being told that your creation can't be licensed in the Experimental Category (homebuilts) and can't be flown.

THE WAG-A-BOND

The Wag-A-Bond, a replica of the Piper Vagabond, is offered with a choice of engines from 65 hp to 115 hp. You can build it as a duplicate of the PA-17, or you may install an O-235 engine and go with the fold-down seat and camper interior, which sleeps two people. The former is called the Wag-A-Bond Classic, while the latter is the Traveler.

The bigger engine gives this airframe Pacer performance, with

Wag-Aero's two-place Wag-A-Bond is based on the Piper PA-17 Vagabond. It is offered in two versions which will accept engines from 65 to 115 hp. With the latter installation it becomes a "Super Vag" and loses much of its charm—and economy. (courtesy Wag-Aero)

a pair of 13-gallon wing tanks for longer range. The Traveler also has doors on both sides, a skylight, and a useful load of 725 pounds (610 pounds for the Classic version).

All Wag-Aero airplanes are covered with Stits Poly-Fiber, a square-weave (same number of threads in both directions) Dacron, and finished in the Stits epoxy paints and fillers, which are top-of-the-line. The fabric covers are offered as pre-sewn envelopes. All the builder has to do is slip them on the airframe components, close the open ends, and shrink to the proper tension with an electric iron. Strangely, the Wag-Aero brochures list a hot air blower for tautening the fabric, while Stits and Ceconite say not to use a hot air gun to tauten the fabric. For best results, use an electric iron, because it allows precise heat control.

THE SPORTSMAN 2 + 2

The Sportsman is a four-placer that uses the Piper PA-12 wing. That means it has no flaps, but it does have spoilers. An optional hinged turtledeck is an idea borrowed from the Piper HE-1 ambulance plane of World War II; it can be used to carry skis and other equipment. Plans for the Sportsman are $89 and consist of 24 pages, each 24 × 36 inches. As with other Wag-Aero designs, you can purchase sub-kits as needed and eventually end up with a complete airplane. Wag-Aero brochures describe the Sportsman as a "shadow of the . . . PA-14 Family Cruiser," but actually it is more airplane than that, with extended wings, 39 gallons of usable fuel, and engines up to 200 hp. The "2+2" indicates that, with rear seats removed and the fold-up turtledeck installed, it will carry two people and provide a cavernous cargo area. This airplane has gull-wing doors on both sides, and a useful load of 1,120 pounds when fitted with the 150-hp O-320 engine.

WAG-AERO PRICES

Sport Trainer. The builder has several options when constructing one of these machines—not only as to the number and types of kits purchased, along with, perhaps, a mix of scrounged Piper components (they all fit), but also with respect to prefabricated and finish-welded components from Wag-Aero. For example, building the Sport Trainer, you may: (1) use a standard Piper J-3 fuselage; (2) order the fuselage materials kit from Wag-Aero for $975 and build a new one yourself; (3) order a tack-welded fuselage from Wag for $2,495 and complete the welding; or (4) purchase a finish-welded

The Wag-Aero Sportsman 2+2 is a "modernized replica" of the Piper PA-14 Family Cruiser, although the Wag-Aero demo airplane is fitted with a 150-hp engine. All Wag-Aero designs are available as plans only, partial kits, or complete kits. (courtesy Wag-Aero)

A Wag-Aero Sportsman 2+2 nearing completion and being fitted with Javelin Aircraft's Ford automobile V-6 engine conversion. (courtesy of Javelin Aircraft, Inc.)

fuselage from Wag-Aero for $3,495.

The basic materials kit for a complete Sport Trainer, less engine, propeller, and covering, is $8,461, and that includes some prefab components such as the tail structure, engine cowling, exhaust

The Javelin Fords—Escort/Lynx four-cylinder, and 230-cu.-in. V-6—have been test flying in a Cessna 150 and Cessna 175, respectively, for several years. For more data, consult *Automobile Engines for Airplanes* (TAB #2447) or contact Javelin Aircraft, Inc. (address in Appendix). (courtesy Javelin Aircraft, Inc.)

system, engine mount, instrument panel, doors, and many fittings. Drawings alone are $65.

The most serious problem when building a Sport Trainer is finding an engine for it under 100 hp. There are no new ones. The original J-3s and PA-11s had 50, 65, and 90 hp. None of these engines are in production today, so a Sport Trainer builder must either search the used market or go to an O-235. Wag-Aero offers a remanufactured O-235-L2C for $7,552 (new, $9,050), but it requires LL100 avgas. So, back to the yellow pages of *Trade-A-Plane*. The O-235s you should be interested in will feed upon automobile unleaded; these are the earlier ones, designed for 80/87 octane fuel.

Wag-A-Bond. A complete materials kit for the Wag-A-Bond Classic is $9,470. The Traveler version, less engine, propeller, and color paint, but including Stits covering and finish up to the color, is $10,437. Drawings are $89.

Here again, you are faced with the problem of finding a proper engine. The Continental C-85 that powers Steven Ogles' Vagabond (Chapter 3), or a C-90, is probably the best compromise between economy and performance. Wagner's demo Wag-A-Bond is fitted with a 115-hp O-235. I certainly would not recommend any more power than that. If you want muscle, it would be better to look at other designs. The Vagabond concept is easily lost in the dust of a lot of horsepower. As it is, the Vagabond just may be, as my wife says, the "funnest" airplane of all the Pipers. Why try to make something else out of it?

Sportsman 2 + 2. This is a four-place airplane, and if you want a four-placer you'll have to pay for it. The complete materials list, including basic flight instruments, is $11,500, less engine, propeller, and wheel pants. A pre-welded fuselage is $3,460 extra, plus a $250 crating charge.

The Wag-Aero Sportsman's empty weight is 60 pounds more than the PA-14's. The Sportsman would get by with one of the O-290s, but the O-320-A2A would probably be the best compromise between economy and performance.

The 150-hp Lycoming O-320-A2A has a compression ratio of 7.00:1 and was designed for 80/87 octane fuel, which means that it can be operated on automobile unleaded gasoline. Wag-Aero prices this engine at $9,596 new, and $7,406 remanufactured.

The 160-hp Lycoming O-320-B2B has a compression ratio of 8.50:1 and requires LL100 blue fuel. It is $9,875 new, and $7,406 remanufactured.

The 180-hp Lycoming O-360-A1A has a compression ratio of 8.50:1, burns LL100 avgas, and is $11,295 new, $8,612 remanufactured.

Sensenich metal propellers for the above are $979 and $1,056.

**Wag-Aero Sport Trainer and Piper PA-11
Specifications and Performance**

	Sport Trainer	Piper PA-11
Engine	C-85	C-90
Fuel capacity (U.S. gal.)	12	18
Wingspan (ft.)	35.3	35.3
Length (ft.)	22.3	22.4
Height (ft.)	6.7	6.7
Empty weight (lbs.)	720	750
Gross weight (lbs.)	1400	1220
Useful load (lbs.)	680	490
Power loading (lbs./hp)	16.5	13.5
Baggage capacity (lbs.)	20	32
Maximum speed (mph)	102	112
Cruising speed (mph)	94	100
Stalling speed (mph)	39	40
Initial climb (fpm)	490	900
Service ceiling (ft.)	12,000	16,000
Cruising range (statute mi.)	220	350

Wag-Aero Sportsman 2 + 2 and Piper PA-14
Specifications and Performance

	Sportsman	Piper PA-14
Engine	150 hp	115 hp
Fuel capacity (U.S. gal.)	39	38
Wingspan (ft.)	35.8	35.5
Length (ft.)	23.4	23.4
Height (ft.)	6.7	6.5
Empty weight (lbs.)	1080	1020
Gross weight (lbs.)	2200	1850
Useful load (lbs.)	1120	830
Power loading (lbs./hp)	14.7	17.1
Baggage capacity (lbs.)	na	80
Maximum speed (mph)	129	123
Cruising speed (mph)	124	110
Stalling speed (mph)	38	46
Initial climb (fpm)	800	600
Service ceiling (ft.)	14,000	12,500
Cruising range (statute mi.)	670	500

Note: Although Wag-Aero appears to think of its four-place Sportsman 2 + 2 as a replica of the four-place Piper PA-14 Family Cruiser, a direct comparison is not very useful because the specification and performance figures given for the Sportsman are for a 150-hp version. The PA-14 was produced with 115 hp.

Wag-Aero Wag-A-Bond and Piper Colt
Specifications and Performance

	Wag-A-Bond	Piper Colt†	Piper PA-17
Engine	115 hp	108 hp	65
Fuel capacity (U.S. gal.)	12	36	12
Wingspan (ft.)	29.3	29.3	29.4
Length (ft.)	18.7	20.2	18.8
Height (ft.)	6	8.3	6.1
Empty weight (lbs.)	725*	940	650
Gross weight (lbs.)	1450*	1650	1150
Useful load (lbs.)	725*	710	500
Power loading (lbs./hp)	12.6*	15.28	17.7
Baggage capacity (lbs.)	60*	100	40
Maximum speed (mph)	136*	120	100
Cruising speed (mph)	124*	108	90
Stalling speed (mph)	45	56	45
Initial climb (fpm)	850*	610	530
Service ceiling (ft.)	na	12,000	10,500
Cruising range (statute mi.)	na	690	250

*Traveler version.

† With 115 horsepower in Wag-Aero's Wag-A-Bond, the closest Piper comparison is the 108-hp Colt.

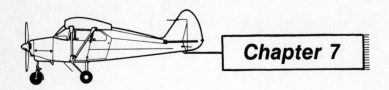

Chapter 7

Refurbishing the Fabric-Covered Pipers

Fabric-covered airplanes continue to be finished in butyrate dope despite the fact that there are superior paints and fillers available which cost no more and are no more difficult to apply. Some cotton fabric is still used despite the fact that a synthetic lasts longer and is stronger, less costly, and no harder to install.

RE-COVERING

Whatever goes on your Piper, it goes on under an STC. The only exception would be a late-model Super Cub re-covered with the Ceconite process—that is, the Ceconite Dacron finished with a cellulose nitrate base under cellulose acetate butyrate dope. Earlier post-World War II Pipers were covered with aircraft-grade cotton fabric finished in butyrate, while prewar models were covered with cotton and finished with the very flammable nitrate dopes.

The point is, all commercially-produced airplanes with fabric covering, including the Pipers, were granted an Approved Type Certificate (ATC) by the CAA/FAA for a complete covering system: fabric, adhesives, tapes, lacing cord, attachment method, filler, and paint. Deviate from that system and you are illegal, unless you employ a modern system that has been awarded a Supplemental Type Certificate (STC).

It is not legal to mix systems; Ceconite fabric finished in Stits Polytone is not legal. The "Dacrons" advertised by aircraft supply houses, which are not part of an approved system, are illegal on an ATCed aircraft.

Re-covering an airplane is not difficult if you understand what is to be done and plan ahead, and you have a proper place to work. We will investigate these requirements, discuss airframe preparation before any fabric goes on, and then look at each STCed system in detail. There are only five of them, including exact duplication of the original.

A problem with re-covering an airplane today is that few FAA people know much about the subject. They tend to depend upon the judgment of the aircraft mechanic with an Inspection Authorization (IA) who "signs-off" the work. More often than not, this is the man who did the work.

If you are not a licensed aircraft mechanic, you may legally do the work yourself if you do so under the "direct supervision" of a licensed mechanic. Make a deal with an IA to come and look at the job when he feels that it is necessary. You really won't take too much of his time, and his fee will be relatively small. If you like to work with your hands, you should seriously consider re-covering your airplane yourself when and if it needs new fabric. Approximately 80 percent of the cost of a new fabric cover is labor. You can get a $3,500 re-cover job for about $750 actual cash outlay—and the job will be done right.

Airframe Preparation

You will start by removing the old fabric, but do not dispose of it; keep in mind while removing it that you may need it for patterns and for reference. It will aid in the location of inspection rings, exit patches for rudder cables, etc., in the new cover.

When positioning drain grommets in the new cover, the old fabric isn't necessarily a good guide. There's not much chance that it is the original. The grommets should be placed at the lowest points of the resting aircraft.

Once the old cover is off, the airplane's structure can be thoroughly cleaned and inspected. It isn't likely that you will ever get another chance to do this, so take your time and do it right.

Check the fuselage tubing for rust and cracks. Especially look for cracks at welds and directly adjacent to welds where the tubing tends to be more brittle due to the welding process. It's best to

The Pipers with spruce wing spars may require revarnishing of the wood, and careful inspection for any sign of moisture deterioration, especially at the butt ends of the spars. If the wood is discolored, check beneath the fittings for incipient rot. With a 10-power magnifying glass, inspect all fittings for cracks.

use a 10× magnifying glass and have the tubing clean, of course. There is always the chance that internal rust may have seriously weakened the structure but has not become visible on the outer surface of the tubing. Low points on the fuselage structure are the most vulnerable to internal rust. A small hole drilled at the low point on each bottom longeron should reveal the presence of moisture inside. The holes may be plugged with self-tapping cadmium screws. Some mechanics probe for suspected internal rust damage with an ice pick. Usually, rust will not be widespread, and a damaged section can be cut out and replaced.

Carefully inspect all fittings, such as those that hold control cable pulleys, landing gear attachments, and tailplane brace wires. Steel fittings that show appreciable rust usually must be replaced. Flat steel plate is very quickly weakened by rust. Check the jackscrew (and its attachment) which controls the position of the horizontal stabilizer. On some of the older airplanes, the jackscrew itself can be so worn that the stabilizer is not adjustable through its full range.

Remove rust/crud/corrosion from aluminum parts with a cleaner such as Stits E-2310 phosphoric acid etch and brightener using a Scotch-Brite pad or aluminum wool. Hand polishing of corroded areas with household abrasives or with metal polish available under Specification MIL-P-6888 is acceptable for use on clad aluminum, but must not be used on anodized aluminum because it will remove the anodized film. Chemical cleaners must be used with care when cleaning an airframe, whatever the structural material. The danger of entrapping corrosive materials in hinge recesses and crevices counteracts any advantage gained for their speed and effectiveness. It is best to use materials that are relatively neutral and easy to remove.

Examine the control system for rusted and/or frayed cables, and check the bellcranks for cracks, proper alignment, and security of attachment. Rotate the pulleys to check for flat spots and free movement.

If it is necessary to replace wiring, hydraulic lines, or fuel lines, make sure that wiring is separated from the hydraulic and fuel lines because a future leak will deteriorate the insulation on the wiring, and an arcing fault in an electric line can ignite the leaking fluid and/or puncture a fuel or hydraulic line to start a serious fire. Where wiring is attached to the structure, inspect for proper clamping of the sustaining grommets.

Chrome moly steel tubing can start to rust overnight if not protected, so it should be sprayed or brushed with a good primer on the same day that it is cleaned and inspected. A zinc chromate or Stits epoxy (Stits epoxy contains a high percentage of zinc chromate) is best. The Stits formula will not "lift" in contact with fabric finishing materials. Other brands require that all parts of the structure that come in contact with doped fabric be covered with cellulose tape or a dope-proof paint. This can be inconvenient if you are attaching fabric to longerons with one of the new cements.

Another consideration at this time is the application of an internal tubing rust inhibitor such as Stits Tubeseal. Fifty years ago, we used linseed oil for this, and as far as I know it worked okay, but there are special formulas for everything nowadays, and I'm sure that Tubeseal is superior to linseed oil. One quart is enough for any of the fabric-covered Pipers.

Tubeseal is applied by drilling a #30 (.128) hole in the top of the tube approximately 1½ inches from an end. Insert 1.5 cc of Tubeseal per foot of one-inch-diameter tubing; 1 cc per foot of ⅝-inch diameter tubing. Close holes with a pop rivet #AD-41H. Rotate the fuselage and let stand at each 90 degrees of rotation for five minutes to assure complete internal coverage.

Wings

Thoroughly clean all metal fittings, such as aileron and flap hinge brackets, strut brackets, and wing attach brackets, then inspect with your magnifying glass for cracks and security of attachment. Carefully inspect the fuel tank installations, including the overflow and drain lines. If yours is a wooden-spar Piper, make sure that there is no moisture present under metal fittings. Clean the wood, because any accumulation of grease or other crud will hold moisture. Picture in your mind where the low areas are when the airplane is at rest; that is, where moisture inside the wing will drain to and collect—along the bottom-front surface of the rear spar, for example, and check for signs of deterioration (or corrosion, if yours is a metal spar). If a section of the wood spar is discolored from moisture, you can probe it gently with a dull-bladed knife to make sure that it is not rotted beneath. Anytime you are in doubt about the airworthiness of any structural member, call in your licensed aircraft mechanic to check out your discovery.

After thoroughly cleaning each bolt, inspect them all with your magnifying glass. Bolts tend to crack in threaded areas and beneath their heads. All bolts must be removed for inspection. Be careful not to crush the wood by overtightening when replacing the bolts.

If internal drag and anti-drag wires are replaced, it will be necessary to carefully square the wing. Mark exact center points at the centerline of each spar where the centerlines of compression members line up. The spars must remain exactly parallel to each other. Some slight shrinkage of the wood may have occurred, so it might be necessary to shim one end of one or more of the compression members. Do not overtighten the drag and anti-drag wires. All that is necessary is to have each individual bay squarely adjusted, and all of the wires as nearly the same tension as possible.

When you are assured that the structure is sound, wood spars should receive a coat of marine spar varnish, and the ribs and fittings can be painted with a zinc chromate primer.

Several major brands of automotive primers are packaged for

aircraft use and labeled as "zinc chromate." When Stits had some of these analyzed, none contained zinc chromate (which is the best corrosion inhibitor). Therefore, a red or black primer should be avoided. The zinc chromate primers, including Stits epoxy, will be yellow with either a green or black tint.

Control Surfaces

The control surface frames should be cleaned, inspected, and given a protective primer coating before re-cover. The dynamic and static balance of the surfaces may not be altered without risk of inducing flutter in flight. Therefore, care must be taken to preserve the center of gravity of each control surface exactly as it was with its original cover and finish. The best way to ensure this is to carefully weigh and determine the CG of each control surface before removing the old fabric.

Ceconite Re-Covering Systems

There are two Ceconite aircraft fabric systems. One is the long-established Dacron cloth finished in butyrate dope; the other (which evolved from Bill Lott's Eonnex Process) is a pretreated Dacron finished in water-based epoxy paints.

Whatever the fabric/finishing system, there are two ways of installing the cloth on the airframe—the "blanket" method, which means that you cut and fit from a roll of fabric, and the use of pre-sewn "envelopes." The envelopes cost more than Dacron by the yard but do save time and labor. A total of 45 yards of 66-inch width is required for the J-3 through PA-14 Pipers, and 40 yards for the PA-15 through PA-22. At this writing, Ceconite Style 102 (2.7 ounces/sq. yd.) is priced at $3.60/sq. yd., which means $162.00 for a J-3 and $144.00 for a Tri-Pacer. Cooper Aviation Supply Company sells J-3 pre-sewn envelopes of Ceconite 102 for $211.25, and $225.60 for a Tri-Pacer. The envelopes are sewn on three sides and slipped on the airframe component like a sock. You close the remaining end and then shrink the cover to its proper tautness with an electric iron.

Actually, the blanket method of covering has become more simplified in recent years because fabric adhesives have been developed—Ceconite's Superbond and Stits' Poly-Tak, for example—which allow the cementing of fabric directly to the airframe, and cemented seams in place of sewn seams.

The original Ceconite system employs Dacrons of either 3.7

ounces/sq. yd. with a strength of 130 pounds per inch width (Style 101), or 2.8 ounces/sq. yd. with tensile strength slightly greater than Grade A aircraft cotton (which is a minimum of 80 pounds per inch width when new). This is Style 102, a standard replacement for cotton fabric.

As originally STCed—an approval that is still valid—the finish procedure begins with nitrate dope (which adheres better to Dacron than does butyrate). The prime and two filler coats are of nitrate dope, followed by three to four coats of clear butyrate, and then two or three coats of aluminum butyrate prior to the final color coats.

In the late 1970s, an alternative finishing procedure was approved employing new epoxies:

1. Two brush coats of Dac-Proofer.

2. Accomplish wing rib-stitching or attachment of screws and washers of fabric to ribs; lay tapes; install grommets.

3. For the buildup coats, spray three cross-coats of Spra-Fill. Thin as necessary. Spra-Fill contains aluminum pigments for ultraviolet protection.

4. Very light sanding with #320 wet-or-dry sandpaper to remove nap (if cotton tapes are used) and any blemishes. If the surface is opaque, proceed with the color coats, or apply another coat of silver Spra-Fill.

5. For a good finish, three color coats are usually needed. For a high-gloss finish, a final spray coat of clear butyrate (which has been supplemented with 10 percent color, reduced equal parts with retarder, and sprayed on) will eliminate the need for rubbing or polishing.

You must achieve dope penetration of fabric and thoroughly coat the Dacron fibers on all sides in order to get mechanical adhesion in addition to the natural adhesion of the dope. Dac-Proofer is preferred as having better adhesive qualities than nitrate or butyrate dope, and is better for step #1, whatever the final finish. Butyrate may be used after step #1, if desired.

Both Ceconite and Stits offer a urethane enamel finish as an alternative, but I don't recommend any kind of enamel on fabric because it is next to impossible to patch and is not sufficiently flexible to prevent cracking.

Charles R. "Bob" Near of Blue River Aircraft Supply is the leading authority on Ceconite's 7600 aircraft fabric system, and I

All of the Dacron fabrics should be tautened with an electric iron after installation on the airframe. Pictured is a special aircraft fabric iron with carefully calibrated heat control, but a household iron is good enough if its temperature can be accurately controlled. (courtesy Blue River Aircraft Supply)

am indebted to him for providing complete data on this unique system.

The system makes use of 3.8 ounce/sq. yd. and 2.8 ounce/sq. yd. Dacrons (Ceconite 76101 and 76102), which are pre-coated with

The rib-stitch pattern is marked in pencil on the tautened fabric, then the reinforcing tapes are applied. (courtesy Blue River Aircraft Supply)

The Ceconite 7600 system employs water-based epoxies, and the finish is applied with a paint pad. These materials are nontoxic, and clean-up is with water. (courtesy Blue River Aircraft Supply)

a thermoset water-borne epoxy ester resin under controlled temperature and pressure.

This cloth is attached to the airframe with a two-part adhesive, heat-tautened with an electric iron, and then, following application of the usual surface tapes, grommets, and inspection rings, the fabric is thoroughly dampened with a sponge wetted in clean water. The water-based filler is then applied with a paint pad or a foam brush. Subsequent coats of this 7601 Filler can be applied with a pad or sprayed. No more than three coats will be required. This filler contains a proven ultraviolet blocking agent, and no silver coatings are needed. The color coats go directly over the 7601 Filler. The color, Flexi-Gloss, is a water-based non-toxic polyurethane that will not support combustion. It is easy to apply, and dries to handle in less than two hours at 77° F.

An important characteristic of aircraft Dacron is that it is tautened by application of heat after it is installed on the airframe, and no further tautening is needed—or desired—by the finishing materials. That is the one drawback to butyrate, including the so-called "non-tautening" butyrates. Over a period of time, the plasticizers in the formula migrate and the butyrates (cellulose acetate butyrate) further tauten.

Stits Poly-Fiber System

The Stits aircraft covering system includes several weights (strengths) of Dacron comparable to those offered by Ceconite, and Poly-Fiber is attached to the airframe in the same time-honored way, as well as by use of Stits Poly-Tak Fabric Cement. The Stits primer, filler, and finish coatings are all epoxy formulas, however, and are truly non-tautening.

After the Poly-Fiber is tautened with an electric iron (set at 250° F for the initial shrinking, 350°F for the final, maximum tension), it should be lightly wiped with a tack cloth to remove any dust and lint particles, then the first coat of Poly-Brush filler is applied. This coating, as the name suggests, is best applied with a brush. It is important to thoroughly fill the weave.

After the first filler coat has set, the wing fabric is attached to the wing ribs. You may use the original method (rib-stitching details are illustrated in the Stits covering manual and FAA AC 43-13, as well as TAB book #2377, *Aircraft Construction, Repair, and Inspection*), screws and washers (on some Pipers), or wire barbs that penetrate the caps of the metal ribs. This last method was originally used on T-crafts and is now permitted by a fairly recent STC.

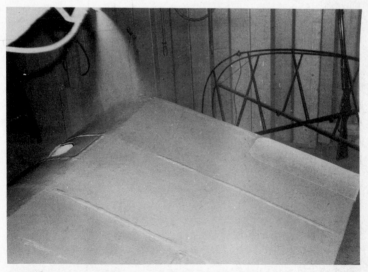

The traditional Ceconite system employs cellulose acetate butyrate (CAB) dope finish, with all but the initial coats sprayed. (courtesy Cooper Aviation Supply Company)

Drain grommets should be installed after all finishing tapes and before the second coat of Poly-Brush is applied.

Three coats of aluminum-pigmented Poly-Spray is sprayed on next, and after that a minimum of two coats of Poly-Tone color. Normally, the final finish coats do not add to the strength or airworthiness of the covering system and are not considered part of the process approved under an STC. However, all of the materials used, from cement through final color, should be of the same system because the solvents of different systems might not be compatible.

Stits Poly-Tone is manufactured from the same generic class of petrochemical feed stock as Poly-Tak, Poly-Brush, and Poly-Spray, and is the standard pigmented finish for the Poly-Fiber Covering Process. The thermo-expansion and elasticity is the same as all sub-coats, and there is no intercoat adhesion problem if the surface is clean. Poly-Tone is non-tautening, non-bleeding, fire retardant, chemical resistant, and is used on both metal and fabric. It air-dries to a satin gloss finish and can be polished to a high luster equal in appearance to any dope or lacquer finish.

A popular option with the Stits system is to complete the Poly-Tone finish through all trim colors, registration numbers, and complete all the inevitable touch-ups for a perfect job. Then clean the surface thoroughly, and immediately shoot two light, wet coats of clear Aero-Thane enamel at 10- to 15-minute intervals. The light film of clear Aero-Thane will produce a gloss superior to any urethane enamel, will smooth all the trim-tape edges, and will provide a finish as durable and as weather-resistant as any pigmented urethane.

Clear Poly-Tone can also be used to give a high-gloss finish. Clear Aero-Thane and clear Poly-Tone have a very light amber shade that may be noticed over light colors.

The original Stits fabrics approved as replacement coverings on aircraft are Styles D-101 and D-103, weighing 3.5 ounces/sq. yd. and 2.6 ounces/sq. yd., respectively, and with strengths of 140 psi and 95 psi. Thread counts are 54×54 and 66×66.

The newest approved fabrics possesses greater thread counts. These are: Style HS150X, weighing 3.0 ounces/sq. yd., 80×80 thread count, and strength of 150 psi, recommended for aircraft with a wing loading of over 12 pounds/sq. ft., and Style HS90X, weighing 1.7 ounces/sq. yd., 94×94 thread count, and strength of 90 psi, approved by the FAA to cover all aircraft regardless of the never-exceed speed or wing loading. The minimum strength requirement for aircraft-grade cotton fabric has always been 80 psi new. Minimum in-service test has always been 56 psi.

Stits Material Estimates. The materials needed for J-3 and other Pipers through the PA-14 include: HS90X fabric, 70-inch width, 45 yards; seven gallons of Poly-Brush; nine gallons of Poly-Spray; seven rolls of 2-inch finishing tape; one roll of 1-inch finishing tape; one spool of rib lacing cord or 250 Martin Fabric Clips (these replace rib-stitching and are available from Cooper Aviation Supply Company); 13 gallons of Poly-Tone; two rolls of ½-inch reinforcing tape; one gallon of Poly-Tak Fabric Cement; and three gallons of Poly-Fiber Reducer.

REPLACEMENT WINDSHIELDS

Windshield installation is a job for an experienced aircraft mechanic. Side windows you may safely do yourself, using the old ones for patterns. Remember that plastics expand and contract more than their metal channels, so try to mount new panels with a ⅛-inch clearance between the plastic and the bottom of the channel.

SHOCK CORD RINGS

The Piper J-5 uses six rubber shock rings in the main landing gear; the Pacer uses only two, and all other fabric-covered Pipers use four. The average price is $16 each. The cloth cover on all shock

Employing the blanket method of covering an airframe, fabric may be cemented to the longerons in four pieces (top, bottom, and each side), and to the wings by installing the cloth spanwise (one piece for the upper surface and one for the lower) and overlapping the cemented seams at the leading and trailing edges. (courtesy Cooper Aviation Supply Company)

rings is color-coded to denote date of manufacture. Ask your mechanic if you are getting fresh ones.

Installation of shock rings is one of the maintenance operations that "the holder of a pilot certificate . . . may perform on any aircraft owned or operated by him . . ." without the supervision of an aircraft mechanic. This is spelled out in FAR Part 43, Appendix A. And it is a mite surprising, because the installation of these rings can be dangerous for the amateur mechanic. This is another job best left to the pros.

FAR Part 43, Appendix A, lists 25 money-saving preventive maintenance operations that pilots and owners may legally perform on their airplanes without an aircraft mechanic's license.

INTERIOR

Most aviation supply houses have a limited selection of upholstery items for the older Pipers. Even Cooper lists headliners only for the PA-12, 18, 20, and 22.

Airtex has the most complete list of such components. Although I can't say much for their service or prices, if you want to order a carpet for a J-4 or a wall panel set for a PA-20, you'll have to address your envelope to Airtex.

TIRES

The 8.00 × 4 tires on the early machines are available from Dresser Tire & Rubber in Los Angeles, Tred Air of California in Bellflower, California, and Midwest Pawnee Center in Vincennes, Indiana.

ENGINES

Be aware that there are two kinds of "zero-time" engines—those overhauled to permissible *service* limits, and those overhauled to *new* limits. There is a significant difference. A *zero-time* engine and an engine with *zero time since major overhaul* are two different things. A brand new engine is, of course, a zero-time engine; so is an engine remanufactured by Continental or Lycoming, which will have a new crankshaft, new cylinders if needed, and whatever is

The 108-horsepower Lycoming O-235. (courtesy AVCO Lycoming)

Specifications
Continental A-50, A-65, A-75, and A-80
(See Figure A)

Cylinder bore (in.)	3⅛
Stroke (in.)	3⅝
Piston displacement (cu. in.)	171
Average dry weight (lbs.)	170
Length (in.)	31
Height (in.)	29⁵⁄₁₆
Width (in.)	31½
Intake valve opens	10° BTC
Intake valve closes	50° ABC
Exhaust valve opens	50° BBC
Exhaust valve closes	15° ATC
Intake valve remains open	240° crankangle
Exhaust valve remains open	245° crankangle
Valve clearance, engine operating	0
Valve clearance, lifters deflated (in.)	.030—.110
Spark plugs, unshielded	Champion C26
Spark plugs, shielded	Champion C26S

Individual Specifications	A-50	A-65	A-75	A-80
Compression ratio.................	5.4:1	6.3:1	6.3:1	7.55:1
Rated rpm........................	1,900	2,300	2,600	2,700
Normal cruise rpm.....:..........	1,800	2,150	2,350	2,450
Max. oil temp (°F)................	215	220	220	220
Max. cyl head temp (°F)...........	550	550	550	550
Min. oil temp takeoff (°F)..........	90	90	90	90
Fuel consumption (gph).............	3.8	4.4	4.8	5.2
Oil pressure @ cruise (psi).........	30—40	30—40	30—40	30—40
Oil sump capacity (qts.)............	4	4	4	4
Oil pressure, idle (lbs.).............	10	10	10	10
Firing order......................	1-3-2-4	1-3-2-4	1-3-2-4	1-3-2-4
Right mag fires upper spark plugs (degrees BTC)........	25	30	29	29
Left mag fires lower spark plugs (degrees BTC)........	28	30	32	32

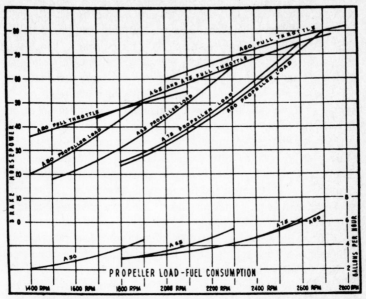

Fig. A. Performance and fuel consumption curves for the A-50, A-65, A-75, and A-80 Continental engines. (courtesy Teledyne Continental Motors)

required to bring all mating parts to the same tolerances as those in a brand new engine. The remanufactured engine will start over with a new log, and it will cost at least a third more than a major overhaul done at an FAA-approved repair station.

An engine receiving a major overhaul at an approved facility may be returned to all new limits, but it will probably cost just as much as remanufacture by the builder, and it will retain its old engine log.

Most major overhauls do not return the engines to new limits throughout, but adhere to the permissible service limits. That might be the best way to go if you have a shop you can trust.

Overhaul to service limits will be in the neighborhood of $3,000 for any of the small Continentals from A-65 through C-90, including installation, with magneto and fuel system overhaul, and new ignition harness. I recently saw this deal priced at $2,787 in *Trade-A-Plane*. The O-235, O-290D, and O-320 will cost $1,000 more.

Continental C-series Engines

Continental's C-series engines, like the A-series, are long out of production, but there is no shortage of parts for them at this writing. As with the A's, dash-numbers and suffix letters indicate variations in accessories. For example, a "-12" following the basic C-75 designation means that a starter generator system is installed. The C-75-12F will have starter, generator, and a flange-type crankshaft. If an "H" is added, that indicates that the crankshaft and crankcase are adapted to feed oil to a controllable-pitch propeller.

Some conversion is possible. A C-75 may be converted to a C-85 rather easily (mostly a matter of changing the carburetor jets), but neither can be made into a C-90 because of the nature and extent of parts differences. Also, you can't convert a dash-8 version (no starter or generator) to a dash-12 because the crankcases are different. One change that is approved and often desirable is the crankshaft. The tapered and flange types are identical except for their exposed ends. Either may be installed in a C-series engine as a replacement.

The shape of the oil sump may differ on some C-series engines, although all are interchangeable. The variation in shape came from a need to adapt the engine to a particular airplane.

All C-series engines produced with carburetors used the Stromberg NA-S3A1 and a gravity feed system. A Marvel-Schebler carburetor was available as an option, as was a fuel-injection system. The fuel-injected engine was identified with a "J" suffix to its dash-number, but neither of these letter versions were delivered in any number.

Eiseman AM-4 magnetos are standard on unshielded ignition systems of the C-85-8 engines. Originally, the C-85-12 models were produced with Eiseman LA-4 mags, but later changed to the Scintilla S4LN-21. The C-90-8 models used the Scintilla S4RN-21, and the C-90-12 employs the Scintilla S4LN-21 magnetos.

Radio-shielded ignition systems require either the Eiseman LA-4 or Scintilla S4LN-21 mags on the dash-12 engines. The Scintilla S4RN-21 mags on the dash-12 engines. The Scintilla S4RN-21 is the only mag available for dash-8 models with radio, because the Eiseman AM-4 is not shielded.

The engine valve action on the C-series and design of the hydraulic valve lifters are similar to that of the A-series engines.

Specifications
Continental C Series
(See Figure B)

	C-75	C-85	C-90
Cylinder bore (in.)	4$\frac{1}{16}$	4$\frac{1}{16}$	4$\frac{1}{16}$
Stroke (in.)	3$\frac{5}{8}$	3$\frac{5}{8}$	3$\frac{5}{8}$
Displacement (cu. in.)	188	188	200.91
Average dry weight (lbs.)		158 to 168	
Intake valve opens (BTC)	8°	8°	15°
Intake valve closes (ABC)	57°	57°	62°
Exhaust valve opens (BBC)	49°	49°	57°
Exhaust valve closes (ATC)	16°	16°	20°
Valve clearance, lifters deflated (in.)	.030-.110	(all models)	
Valve clearance, engine operating (in.)	0	0	0
Compression ratio	6.3:1	6.3:1	7.00:1
Rated rpm	2,275	2,575	2,475
Maximum oil temp (°F)	220	220	225
Minimum oil temp, takeoff (°F)	75	75	75
Cruise oil pressure (psi)	30—35	30—35	30-35
Minimum idle oil pressure (psi)	10	10	10
Oil sump capacity, (qts.)	4	4	4.8
Firing order	1-3-2-4	1-3-2-4	1-3-2-4
R mag fires (BTC)	28°	28°	26°
L mag fires (BTC)	30°	30°	28°
Length (in.)	31.25	31.25	31.25
Height (in.)	24.19	24.19	24.19
Width (in.)	31.50	31.50	31.50

Note: The Continental C-90 was also rated at 95 hp @ 2,625 rpm.

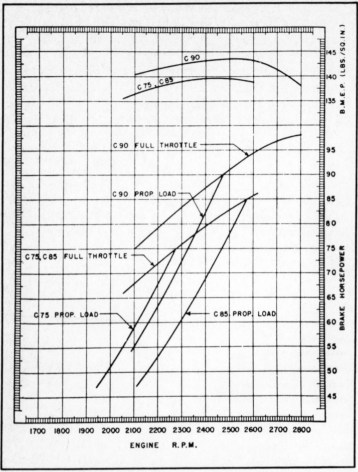

Fig. B. Horsepower vs. rpm at full throttle and at propeller load, Continental engines C-75, C-85, and C-90. (courtesy Teledyne Continental Motors)

Lycoming Engines

The cast aluminum crankcases of Lycomings and Continentals are made in two halves and mated at the engines' vertical centerlines. The finned cylinder barrels are machined from steel forgings, to which the cast aluminum heads are screwed and shrunk. Crankshafts are forged steel and have a separate throw for each rod and piston, with main bearings between each pair of throws. The main bearing housings are integral with the crankcases in both Lycomings and Continentals.

128

The Lycomings have their camshafts and pushrods above the crankshaft, while the Continentals have theirs below. On the higher horsepower engines, Lycoming uses sodium-filled exhaust valves for even heat dissipation, while Continentals have caps on their valve stems which cause the valves to slowly rotate for this purpose. One significant difference is that the Lycs run the intake manifold through the crankcase (oil sump). Also, the low-horsepower Lycomings did not receive hydraulic valve lifters until the O-290-D2 appeared.

Specifications
Lycoming O-145

	O-145-A	O-145-B	O-145-C
Cylinder bore (in.)	3⅝	3⅝	3⅝
Stroke (in.)	3½	3½	3½
Displacement (cu. in.)	144.5	144.5	144.5
Compression ratio	5.65:1	6.5:1	6.5:1
Rated rpm	2,300	2,550	3,100
Cruising rpm	2,150	2,450	2,850
Rated horsepower	55	65	75
Average dry weight (lbs.)	163	163	163
Oil pressure, normal (psi)	55—80	55—80	55—80
Oil pressure, idle (psi)	15	15	15
Valve clearance, cold, both (in.)	.015	.015	.015
Spark advance (BTC)	20°	20°	25°
Firing order	1-3-2-4	1-3-2-4	1-3-2-4
Magnetos	Scintilla SF-4L (all models)		

Lycoming O-235 and O-290. The first O-235 appeared in 1941 as power for the Piper J-5C Cub Cruiser. It was rated at 100 hp. After World War II, this engine was again offered at 100 hp, but a 108-hp version soon appeared, followed later by the 115-hp model. The O-290-D, rated at 125 hp, was first fitted to the Piper YL-14 in 1944. The O-290-Ds and D2s were Piper Pacer, Tri-Pacer, and Super Cub engines.

There are four popular versions of the O-290-D, all of them designed for 80-octane fuel. Of the more than 20 versions of the O-235,

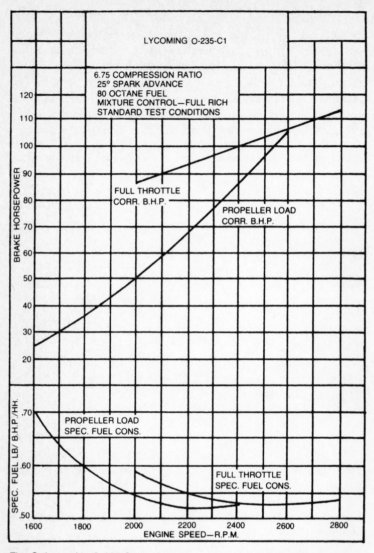

Fig. C. Lycoming O-235-C1 performance chart. (courtesy AVCO Lycoming)

all of the 100-hp and 108-hp versions use 80 octane, plus the following 115-hp models: O-235-C1, -C1B, -C2A, -C2B, -C2C, -E1, -E1B, -E2A, and -E2B. All of these have a 6.75:1 compression ratio, and all are rated at 2,800 rpm.

The O-235-C series employs the Marvel-Schebler MA-3A carburetor. The O-290-D uses the Marvel-Schebler MA-3SPA

Specifications
Lycoming O-235-C and O-290-D
(See Figure C)

	O-23-C	O-290-D
Cylinder bore (in.)	4.375	4.875
Stroke (in.)	3.875	3.875
Displacement (cu. in.)	233.3	289
Compression ratio	6.75:1	6.50:1
Rated rpm	2,600	2,600
Cruising rpm	2,350	2,350
Rated horsepower	108	125
Dry weight (lbs.)	240	263
Oil pressure, normal (psi)	65—85	65—85
Oil pressure, idle (psi)	25	25
Tappet setting, cold (in.)	.010	.010
Spark advance (BTC)	25°	25°

carburetor.

Both the O-235 and the O-290-D use the Scintilla S4LN-20 magneto on the right, and a S4LN-21 on the left. Left mags on both engines are impulse-coupled; that is, they have a spring-loaded device that retards the spark at cranking rpm allowing the mag to fire at TDC. When the engine is revved past 300-400 rpm, the impulse coupler disengages and the mag fires at its normal BTC position.

On both engine series, the upper plugs on the right side of the engine are fired by the right mag; and the bottom plugs on the right side are fired by the left mag. The top plugs on the left side are fired by the left mag, and the bottom plugs on the left side are fired by the right magneto.

Both the O-235-C and the O-290-D have a mounting pad, just ahead of the #1 cylinder, which is intended for installation of a hydraulic valve to operate a controllable-pitch propeller. Such a valve allows engine oil, under pressure, to flow through the hollow crankshaft to the blade-rotating mechanism of the prop. Installation of this valve requires the removal of the Welch-type expansion plug in the front of the crankshaft.

The O-290-D2 is rated at 135 hp, its ten extra horsepower gained through an increase in compression ratio to 7.5:1. This engine employs a heavier piston than that used in the O-290-D, and also goes to hydraulic tappets and a larger intake valve. Another important difference is that spark advance is 18° BTC for the O-290-D2.

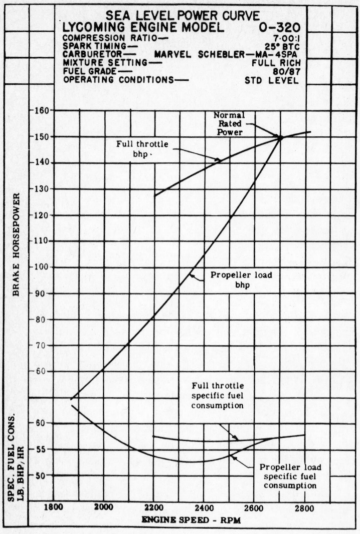

Fig. D. Lycoming O-320 performance chart. (courtesy AVCO Lycoming)

Lycoming O-320. The O-320 engines also have provision in the crankcase, ahead of the #1 cylinder, for a hydraulic propeller. The O-320 in the used market may or may not have chromed cylinder barrels. Make sure that you *never* put chromed piston rings in a chromed cylinder barrel.

Specifications
Lycoming O-320-A
(See Figure D)

Cylinder bore (in.)........................	5.125
Stroke (in.)..............................	3.875
Piston displacement (cu. in.)................	319.8
Compression ratio........................	7.00:1
Rated rpm...............................	2,700
Rated horsepower........................	150
Cruising rpm.............................	2,450
Dry weight (lbs.).........................	268
Oil pressure, normal (psi).................	65 to 85
Oil pressure, idle minimum (psi)...........	25
Oil sump capacity (qts.)...................	8
Fuel grade, octane........................	80/87
Spark advance (BTC)......................	25°
Tappet setting, cold engine (in.)............	.028—.080

The O-320 Lycomings have an ignition system similar to that of the O-235 and O-290-D engines, and most also employ the Scintilla S4LN-20 and -21 magnetos. The induction system, too, is practically the same, except that the O-320 is equipped with a Marvel-Schebler MA-4SPA carburetor.

There are more than 50 versions of the O-320, some of which had significant AD notices against them. Therefore, if you are planning to replace a lower horsepower engine with an O-320, check with your mechanic to make sure that you are getting a proper one, and one that will feed upon the kind of fuel you prefer to use. The O-320-A through -A3Cs are rated at 150 hp at 2,700 rpm with 80/87 octane.

The 160-hp O-320-D1F and -D2F also burn 80/87, as do all of the E suffixes through O-320-E1H. (All of the E suffixes are 150 hp, although the -E2A and -E2C are alternately rated at 140 hp at 2,450 rpm.)

Your mechanic will have a bulletin from Lycoming that allows field conversions of the O-320-B1A through -B3C to 80/87 fuel. The engines thus converted are designated -C1A through -C3C models.

Specifications
Lycoming O-360-A

Cylinder bore (in.)	5.125
Stroke (in.)	4.375
Piston displacement (cu. in.)	361.0
Compression ratio	8.5:1
Rated horsepower	180
Rated rpm	2,700
Firing order	1-3-2-4
Spark advance (BTC)	25°
Valve clearance, hydraulic lifters flat (in.)	.028—.080

Lycoming O-360. If you are contemplating the installation of an O-360 in place of a less powerful engine, be advised that some of these very popular engines had some teething problems and some expensive AD notes against them, so consult your mechanic on this question. Also, be prepared to pay more for maintenance, fuel, and overhaul.

Last time I counted, there were 86 different versions of the O-360, 27 of them 180-hp carbureted models. The float-type carburetors used are the Marvel-Schebler MA-4-5 and HA-6 (which are single-barrel with manual mixture control) and the Marvel-Schebler MA-4-5AA (also single barrel, but with automatic pressure altitude mixture control). The Bendix-Stromberg PSH-5BD carburetor is pressure-operated, with a single horizontal barrel, incorporating an airflow-operated power enrichment valve and an automatic mixture control unit. It also has a manual mixture control that works independently of, and in parallel with, the automatic mixture control. Chances are, however, that you will consider only a rebuilt O-360-A1A version, which uses the MA-4-5 carburetor and S4LN-20 and -21 magnetos.

All models of the O-360 use 100-octane fuel (except the rare 168-hp O-360-B1A through -B2B versions, designed for 80/87 fuel). The dry weight of these engines, including mags, carburetor, ignition harness, engine baffles, spark plugs, tach drive, starter, and generator or alternator, ranges from 282 to 290 pounds. The 200-hp models are heavier, the turbocharged, fuel-injected TIO-360 weighing a hefty 386 pounds.

The O-360s range in length from 29.56 to 30.7 inches, and are 24.59 inches in height and 33.37 inches in width.

Engine Costs

The following are sample costs for major overhauls and new and remanufactured engines. New and remanufactured prices are from Wag-Aero. Major-overhaul prices are averages taken from ads in *Trade-A-Plane* at the time of this writing.

Model	Major Overhaul	Remanufactured	New
O-235-1C	$3,600—$4,000	$7,552	$9,050
O-320-A2A	3,600— 4,000	7,406	9,595
O-360-A1A	3,750— 4,450	8,612	11,295
A-65/C-90	2,800— 3,500		

Appendix:
Suppliers, Clubs,
and Other Helpful Addresses

Aircraft Maintenance & Engineering
R.D. 1
Olean Airport
Hinsdale, NY 14743
(716) 968-1159
Engine overhaul

Aircraft Supply
Allegheny County Airport
West Mifflin, PA 15122
(800) 245-0690
(412) 462-8200
Batteries, tires, etc.

Aircraftsmen, Inc.
Cambridge Municipal Airport
Cambridge, MD 21613
(301) 221-0200
Engine overhaul

Airtex Products, Inc.
259 Lower Morrisville Rd.
Fallsington, PA 19054
(215) 295-4115
Aircraft interiors

Avco Lycoming
Williamsport, PA 17701
(717) 323-6181
Engine manufacturer

AWK Aviation
5539 West 142nd Pl.
Hawthorne, CA 90250
Aircraft checklists

Blue River Aircraft Supply
P.O. Box 91
Harvard, NE 68944
(402) 772-3651
Ceconite 7600 fabric system

Carter Aircraft Engines, Inc.
2116 West G St.
Elizabethton, TN 37643
(800) 251-7050
(615) 542-2811
Engine overhaul

Cooper Aviation Supply Co.
Superflite Division
2149 East Pratt Blvd.
Elk Grove Village, IL 60007
(800) 323-0611
(312) 364-2600
Ceconite systems, windshields

Dresser Tire & Rubber Co.
6208 South Alameda
P.O. Box 01736
Los Angeles, CA 90001
Tires and tubes

Experimental Aircraft Assoc.
Wittman Airfield
Oshkosh, WI 54903
(414) 426-4800
Automobile fuel STCs

Hower Aviation
7879 Bradenton Rd.
Sarasota, FL 34243
(813) 355-5237
Fabric systems, windshields

Javelin Aircraft, Inc.
Mr. David Blanton
Augusta Municipal Airport
Augusta, KS 67230
(316) 733-1011
Car engine conversions

Midwest Pawnee Center
P.O. Box 234
Vincennes, IN 47591
Tires, batteries, fabric, etc.

Petersen Aviation, Inc.
Route 1, Box 18
Minden, NE 68959
(308) 832-2200
Automobile fuel STCs

Short Wing Piper Club
Route #11
708 W. Annie Dr.
Munice, IN 47302
(317) 298-5487 evenings

Skyward Supply
P.O. Box 23342
Stanley, KS 66223
(800) 445-0670
Windshields, tires, etc.

Stits Aircraft Coatings
P.O. Box 3084
Riverside, CA 92509
(714) 684-4280
Stits fabric-finishing system

Sun Country Aviation
7602 Boeing Ave.
El Paso, TX 79925
(915) 778-5316
Engine overhaul

Teledyne Continental Motors
Aircraft Products Division
P.O. Box 90
Mobile, AL 36601
(205) 438-3411
Engine manufacturer

Trade-A-Plane
Crossville, TN 38555
(615) 484-5137
Trade newspaper

Tred Air of California
9040 E. Rosecrans Ave.
Bellflower, CA 90706
(213) 630-6223
Tires and tubes

Univair Aircraft Corp.
2500 Himalaya Road
Aurora, CO 80011
(303) 364-7661
Parts for classics

Wag-Aero
Box 181
1216 North Road
Lyons, WI 53148
(414) 763-9586
Piper replicas and parts

Index

Other Bestsellers From TAB

Other Bestsellers From TAB

☐ **FLYING VFR IN MARGINAL WEATHER**
—2nd Edition—Paul Garrison, Revised by Norval Kennedy

In this revised edition, you'll find technological information on such weather phenomena as wind shear . . . details on today's most advanced lightplane instrumentation including altimeters, airspeed indicators, vertical speed indicators, turn-and-bank indicators, and more . . . tips on the use of wing levelers and autopilots—. . . and a practical look at the most advanced new technology in VHF navigation receivers, OBIs, and other navigation equipment including Loran C. 224 pp., 91 illus.
Paper $14.95   Hard $21.95
Book No. 2416

☐ **THE CESSNA 172**
—Bill Clarke

If you're the owner of a Cessna 172, a prospective owner, pilot, dealer, service or maintenance person, or anyone else who needs a quick reference to Cessnas . . . you'll find all the information you need conveniently gathered together and clearly presented in this buyer's guide. It supplies all the background knowledge on these airplanes that you need to make a wise purchase, new or used, to improve the performance and comfort of your Cessna, to make sure it meets all the FAA requirements, and to keep it running safely and smoothly for years. 320 pp., 113 illus.
Paper $12.95   Hard $19.95
Book No. 2412

☐ **AVIATION: A COMPLETE LEGAL GUIDE**
—Cliff Roberson, LLM, Ph.D.

Discover the answers to almost any legal question concerning private flying or civil aviation. Written in easy-to-follow layman's language, you'll find a comprehensive overview of the obligations and liabilities that federal, state, and local laws place on pilots, aircraft owners, maintenance personnel, flight operators, flight instructors, homebuilders, and even ultralight flyers. 210 pp., 65 illus.
Paper $12.95   Hard $19.95
Book No. 2414

☐ **THE AVIATORS'S GUIDE TO MODERN NAVIGATION**
—Donald J. Clausing

From simple dead reckoning and the old standbys such as ADF and other NDBs . . . to the familiar VOR-based systems . . . to the more advanced LORAN-C, Omega/VLF, and inertial navigation . . . to the satellite based NAVSTAR which will be in place by the end of the decade! The wealth of professional tips, advice, and instruction included will show you how to simplify navigation and make it more accurate at the same time! 288 pp., 124 illus.
Paper $17.95   Hard $26.95
Book No. 2408

Other Bestsellers From TAB